The Poetry of Algernon Charles Swinburne

VOLUME XV - ASTROPHEL & OTHER POEMS

Algernon Charles Swinburne was born on April 5th, 1837, in London, into a wealthy Northumbrian family. He was educated at Eton and at Balliol College, Oxford, but did not complete a degree.

In 1860 Swinburne published two verse dramas but achieved his first literary success in 1865 with Atalanta in Calydon, written in the form of classical Greek tragedy. The following year "Poems and Ballads" brought him instant notoriety. He was now identified with "indecent" themes and the precept of art for art's sake.

Although he produced much after this success in general his popularity and critical reputation declined. The most important qualities of Swinburne's work are an intense lyricism, his intricately extended and evocative imagery, metrical virtuosity, rich use of assonance and alliteration, and bold, complex rhythms.

Swinburne's physical appearance was small, frail, and plagued by several other oddities of physique and temperament. Throughout the 1860s and 1870s he drank excessively and was prone to accidents that often left him bruised, bloody, or unconscious. Until his forties he suffered intermittent physical collapses that necessitated removal to his parents' home while he recovered.

Throughout his career Swinburne also published literary criticism of great worth. His deep knowledge of world literatures contributed to a critical style rich in quotation, allusion, and comparison. He is particularly noted for discerning studies of Elizabethan dramatists and of many English and French poets and novelists. As well he was a noted essayist and wrote two novels.

In 1879, Swinburne's friend and literary agent, Theodore Watts-Dunton, intervened during a time when Swinburne was dangerously ill. Watts-Dunton isolated Swinburne at a suburban home in Putney and gradually weaned him from alcohol, former companions and many other habits as well.

Much of his poetry in this period may be inferior but some individual poems are exceptional; "By the North Sea," "Evening on the Broads," "A Nympholept," "The Lake of Gaube," and "Neap-Tide."

Swinburne lived another thirty years with Watts-Dunton. He denied Swinburne's friends access to him, controlled the poet's money, and restricted his activities. It is often quoted that 'he saved the man but killed the poet'.

Swinburne died on April 10th, 1909 at the age of seventy-two.

Index of Contents

ASTROPHEL AND OTHER POEMS

TO WILLIAM MORRIS

ASTROPHEL

AFTER READING SIR PHILIP SIDNEY'S ARCADIA IN THE GARDEN OF AN OLD ENGLISH MANOR HOUSE

I

A star in the silence that follows
The song of the death of the sun
Speaks music in heaven, and the hollows
And heights of the world are as one;
One lyre that outsings and outlightens
The rapture of sunset, and thrills
Mute night till the sense of it brightens
The soul that it fills.

The flowers of the sun that is sunken
Hang heavy of heart as of head;
The bees that have eaten and drunken
The soul of their sweetness are fled;
But a sunflower of song, on whose honey
My spirit has fed as a bee,
Makes sunnier than morning was sunny
The twilight for me.

The letters and lines on the pages
That sundered mine eyes and the flowers
Wax faint as the shadows of ages
That sunder their season and ours;
As the ghosts of the centuries that sever
A season of colourless time
From the days whose remembrance is ever,
As they were, sublime.

The season that bred and that cherished
The soul that I commune with yet,
Had it utterly withered and perished
To rise not again as it set,
Shame were it that Englishmen living
Should read as their forefathers read
The books of the praise and thanksgiving
Of Englishmen dead.

O light of the land that adored thee
And kindled thy soul with her breath,
Whose life, such as fate would afford thee,
Was lovelier than aught but thy death,
By what name, could thy lovers but know it,
Might love of thee hail thee afar,
Philisides, Astrophel, poet
Whose love was thy star?

A star in the moondawn of Maytime,
A star in the cloudland of change;
Too splendid and sad for the daytime
To cheer or eclipse or estrange;
Too sweet for tradition or vision
To see but through shadows of tears
Rise deathless across the division
Of measureless years.

The twilight may deepen and harden
As nightward the stream of it runs
Till starshine transfigure a garden
Whose radiance responds to the sun's:
The light of the love of thee darkens
The lights that arise and that set:
The love that forgets thee not hearkens
If England forget.

II

Bright and brief in the sight of grief and love the light of thy lifetime shone,
Seen and felt by the gifts it dealt, the grace it gave, and again was gone:
Ay, but now it is death, not thou, whom time has conquered as years pass on.

Ay, not yet may the land forget that bore and loved thee and praised and wept,
Sidney, lord of the stainless sword, the name of names that her heart's love kept
Fast as thine did her own, a sign to light thy life till it sank and slept.

Bright as then for the souls of men thy brave Arcadia resounds and shines,
Lit with love that beholds above all joys and sorrows the steadfast signs,
Faith, a splendour that hope makes tender, and truth, whose presage the soul divines.

All the glory that girds the story of all thy life as with sunlight round,
All the spell that on all souls fell who saw thy spirit, and held them bound,
Lives for all that have heard the call and cadence yet of its music sound.

Music bright as the soul of light, for wings an eagle, for notes a dove,

Leaps and shines from the lustrous lines wherethrough thy soul from afar above
Shone and sang till the darkness rang with light whose fire is the fount of love.

Love that led thee alive, and fed thy soul with sorrows and joys and fears,
Love that sped thee, alive and dead, to fame's fair goal with thy peerless peers,
Feeds the flame of thy quenchless name with light that lightens the rayless years.

Dark as sorrow though night and morrow may lower with presage of clouded fame,
How may she that of old bare thee, may Sidney's England, be brought to shame?
How should this be, while England is? What need of answer beyond thy name?

III

From the love that transfigures thy glory,
From the light of the dawn of thy death,
The life of thy song and thy story
Took subtler and fierier breath.
And we, though the day and the morrow
Set fear and thanksgiving at strife,
Hail yet in the star of thy sorrow
The sun of thy life.

Shame and fear may beset men here, and bid thanksgiving and pride be dumb:
Faith, discrowned of her praise, and wound about with toils till her life wax numb,
Scarce may see if the sundawn be, if darkness die not and dayrise come.

But England, enmeshed and benetted
With spiritless villainies round,
With counsels of cowardice fretted,
With trammels of treason enwound,
Is yet, though the season be other
Than wept and rejoiced over thee,
Thine England, thy lover, thy mother,
Sublime as the sea.

Hers wast thou: if her face be now less bright, or seem for an hour less brave,
Let but thine on her darkness shine, thy saviour spirit revive and save,
Time shall see, as the shadows flee, her shame entombed in a shameful grave.

If death and not life were the portal
That opens on life at the last,
If the spirit of Sidney were mortal
And the past of it utterly past,
Fear stronger than honour was ever,
Forgetfulness mightier than fame,
Faith knows not if England should never
Subside into shame.

Yea, but yet is thy sun not set, thy sunbright spirit of trust withdrawn:
England's love of thee burns above all hopes that darken or fears that fawn:
Hers thou art: and the faithful heart that hopes begets upon darkness dawn.

The sunset that sunrise will follow
Is less than the dream of a dream:
The starshine on height and on hollow
Sheds promise that dawn shall redeem:
The night, if the daytime would hide it,
Shows lovelier, aflame and afar,
Thy soul and thy Stella's beside it,
A star by a star.

A NYMPHOLEPT

Summer, and noon, and a splendour of silence, felt,
Seen, and heard of the spirit within the sense.
Soft through the frondage the shades of the sunbeams melt,
Sharp through the foliage the shafts of them, keen and dense,
Cleave, as discharged from the string of the God's bow, tense
As a war-steed's girth, and bright as a warrior's belt.
Ah, why should an hour that is heaven for an hour pass hence?

I dare not sleep for delight of the perfect hour,
Lest God be wroth that his gift should be scorned of man.
The face of the warm bright world is the face of a flower,
The word of the wind and the leaves that the light winds fan
As the word that quickened at first into flame, and ran,
Creative and subtle and fierce with invasive power,
Through darkness and cloud, from the breath of the one God, Pan.

The perfume of earth possessed by the sun pervades
The chaster air that he soothes but with sense of sleep.
Soft, imminent, strong as desire that prevails and fades,
The passing noon that beholds not a cloudlet weep
Imbues and impregnates life with delight more deep
Than dawn or sunset or moonrise on lawns or glades
Can shed from the skies that receive it and may not keep.

The skies may hold not the splendour of sundown fast;
It wanes into twilight as dawn dies down into day.
And the moon, triumphant when twilight is overpast,
Takes pride but awhile in the hours of her stately sway.
But the might of the noon, though the light of it pass away,
Leaves earth fulfilled of desires and of dreams that last;

But if any there be that hath sense of them none can say.

For if any there be that hath sight of them, sense, or trust
Made strong by the might of a vision, the strength of a dream,
His lips shall straiten and close as a dead man's must,
His heart shall be sealed as the voice of a frost-bound stream.
For the deep mid mystery of light and of heat that seem
To clasp and pierce dark earth, and enkindle dust,
Shall a man's faith say what it is? or a man's guess deem?

Sleep lies not heavier on eyes that have watched all night
Than hangs the heat of the noon on the hills and trees.
Why now should the haze not open, and yield to sight
A fairer secret than hope or than slumber sees?
I seek not heaven with submission of lips and knees,
With worship and prayer for a sign till it leap to light:
I gaze on the gods about me, and call on these.

I call on the gods hard by, the divine dim powers
Whose likeness is here at hand, in the breathless air,
In the pulseless peace of the fervid and silent flowers,
In the faint sweet speech of the waters that whisper there.
Ah, what should darkness do in a world so fair?
The bent-grass heaves not, the couch-grass quails not or cowers;
The wind's kiss frets not the rowan's or aspen's hair.

But the silence trembles with passion of sound suppressed,
And the twilight quivers and yearns to the sunward, wrung
With love as with pain; and the wide wood's motionless breast
Is thrilled with a dumb desire that would fain find tongue
And palpitates, tongueless as she whom a man-snake stung,
Whose heart now heaves in the nightingale, never at rest
Nor satiated ever with song till her last be sung.

Is it rapture or terror that circles me round, and invades
Each vein of my life with hope—if it be not fear?
Each pulse that awakens my blood into rapture fades,
Each pulse that subsides into dread of a strange thing near
Requickens with sense of a terror less dread than dear.
Is peace not one with light in the deep green glades
Where summer at noonday slumbers? Is peace not here?

The tall thin stems of the firs, and the roof sublime
That screens from the sun the floor of the steep still wood,
Deep, silent, splendid, and perfect and calm as time,
Stand fast as ever in sight of the night they stood,
When night gave all that moonlight and dewfall could.
The dense ferns deepen, the moss glows warm as the thyme:

The wild heath quivers about me: the world is good.

Is it Pan's breath, fierce in the tremulous maidenhair,
That bids fear creep as a snake through the woodlands, felt
In the leaves that it stirs not yet, in the mute bright air,
In the stress of the sun? For here has the great God dwelt:
For hence were the shafts of his love or his anger dealt.
For here has his wrath been fierce as his love was fair,
When each was as fire to the darkness its breath bade melt.

Is it love, is it dread, that enkindles the trembling noon,
That yearns, reluctant in rapture that fear has fed,
As man for woman, as woman for man? Full soon,
If I live, and the life that may look on him drop not dead,
Shall the ear that hears not a leaf quake hear his tread,
The sense that knows not the sound of the deep day's tune
Receive the God, be it love that he brings or dread.

The naked noon is upon me: the fierce dumb spell,
The fearful charm of the strong sun's imminent might,
Unmerciful, steadfast, deeper than seas that swell,
Pervades, invades, appals me with loveless light,
With harsher awe than breathes in the breath of night.
Have mercy, God who art all! For I know thee well,
How sharp is thine eye to lighten, thine hand to smite.

The whole wood feels thee, the whole air fears thee: but fear
So deep, so dim, so sacred, is wellnigh sweet.
For the light that hangs and broods on the woodlands here,
Intense, invasive, intolerant, imperious, and meet
To lighten the works of thine hands and the ways of thy feet,
Is hot with the fire of the breath of thy life, and dear
As hope that shrivels or shrinks not for frost or heat.

Thee, thee the supreme dim godhead, approved afar,
Perceived of the soul and conceived of the sense of man,
We scarce dare love, and we dare not fear: the star
We call the sun, that lit us when life began
To brood on the world that is thine by his grace for a span,
Conceals and reveals in the semblance of things that are
Thine immanent presence, the pulse of thy heart's life, Pan.

The fierce mid noon that wakens and warms the snake
Conceals thy mercy, reveals thy wrath: and again
The dew-bright hour that assuages the twilight brake
Conceals thy wrath and reveals thy mercy: then
Thou art fearful only for evil souls of men
That feel with nightfall the serpent within them wake,

And hate the holy darkness on glade and glen.

Yea, then we know not and dream not if ill things be,
Or if aught of the work of the wrong of the world be thine.
We hear not the footfall of terror that treads the sea,
We hear not the moan of winds that assail the pine:
We see not if shipwreck reign in the storm's dim shrine;
If death do service and doom bear witness to thee
We see not,—know not if blood for thy lips be wine.

But in all things evil and fearful that fear may scan,
As in all things good, as in all things fair that fall,
We know thee present and latent, the lord of man;
In the murmuring of doves, in the clamouring of winds that call
And wolves that howl for their prey; in the midnight's pall,
In the naked and nymph-like feet of the dawn, O Pan,
And in each life living, O thou the God who art all.

Smiling and singing, wailing and wringing of hands,
Laughing and weeping, watching and sleeping, still
Proclaim but and prove but thee, as the shifted sands
Speak forth and show but the strength of the sea's wild will
That sifts and grinds them as grain in the storm-wind's mill.
In thee is the doom that falls and the doom that stands:
The tempests utter thy word, and the stars fulfil.

Where Etna shudders with passion and pain volcanic
That rend her heart as with anguish that rends a man's,
Where Typho labours, and finds not his thews Titanic,
In breathless torment that ever the flame's breath fans,
Men felt and feared thee of old, whose pastoral clans
Were given to the charge of thy keeping; and soundless panic
Held fast the woodland whose depths and whose heights were Pan's.

And here, though fear be less than delight, and awe
Be one with desire and with worship of earth and thee,
So mild seems now thy secret and speechless law,
So fair and fearless and faithful and godlike she,
So soft the spell of thy whisper on stream and sea,
Yet man should fear lest he see what of old men saw
And withered: yet shall I quail if thy breath smite me.

Lord God of life and of light and of all things fair,
Lord God of ravin and ruin and all things dim,
Death seals up life, and darkness the sunbright air,
And the stars that watch blind earth in the deep night swim
Laugh, saying, "What God is your God, that ye call on him?
What is man, that the God who is guide of our way should care

If day for a man be golden, or night be grim?"

But thou, dost thou hear? Stars too but abide for a span,
Gods too but endure for a season; but thou, if thou be
God, more than shadows conceived and adored of man,
Kind Gods and fierce, that bound him or made him free,
The skies that scorn us are less in thy sight than we,
Whose souls have strength to conceive and perceive thee, Pan,
With sense more subtle than senses that hear and see.

Yet may not it say, though it seek thee and think to find
One soul of sense in the fire and the frost-bound clod,
What heart is this, what spirit alive or blind,
That moves thee: only we know that the ways we trod
We tread, with hands unguided, with feet unshod,
With eyes unlightened; and yet, if with steadfast mind,
Perchance may we find thee and know thee at last for God.

Yet then should God be dark as the dawn is bright,
And bright as the night is dark on the world—no more.
Light slays not darkness, and darkness absorbs not light;
And the labour of evil and good from the years of yore
Is even as the labour of waves on a sunless shore.
And he who is first and last, who is depth and height,
Keeps silence now, as the sun when the woods wax hoar.

The dark dumb godhead innate in the fair world's life
Imbues the rapture of dawn and of noon with dread,
Infects the peace of the star-shod night with strife,
Informs with terror the sorrow that guards the dead.
No service of bended knee or of humbled head
May soothe or subdue the God who has change to wife:
And life with death is as morning with evening wed.

And yet, if the light and the life in the light that here
Seem soft and splendid and fervid as sleep may seem
Be more than the shine of a smile or the flash of a tear,
Sleep, change, and death are less than a spell-struck dream,
And fear than the fall of a leaf on a starlit stream.
And yet, if the hope that hath said it absorb not fear,
What helps it man that the stars and the waters gleam?

What helps it man, that the noon be indeed intense,
The night be indeed worth worship? Fear and pain
Were lords and masters yet of the secret sense,
Which now dares deem not that light is as darkness, fain
Though dark dreams be to declare it, crying in vain.
For whence, thou God of the light and the darkness, whence

Dawns now this vision that bids not the sunbeams wane?

What light, what shadow, diviner than dawn or night,
Draws near, makes pause, and again—or I dream—draws near?
More soft than shadow, more strong than the strong sun's light,
More pure than moonbeams—yea, but the rays run sheer
As fire from the sun through the dusk of the pinewood, clear
And constant; yea, but the shadow itself is bright
That the light clothes round with love that is one with fear.

Above and behind it the noon and the woodland lie,
Terrible, radiant with mystery, superb and subdued,
Triumphant in silence; and hardly the sacred sky
Seems free from the tyrannous weight of the dumb fierce mood
Which rules as with fire and invasion of beams that brood
The breathless rapture of earth till its hour pass by
And leave her spirit released and her peace renewed.

I sleep not: never in sleep has a man beholden
This. From the shadow that trembles and yearns with light
Suppressed and elate and reluctant—obscure and golden
As water kindled with presage of dawn or night—
A form, a face, a wonder to sense and sight,
Grows great as the moon through the month; and her eyes embolden
Fear, till it change to desire, and desire to delight.

I sleep not: sleep would die of a dream so strange;
A dream so sweet would die as a rainbow dies,
As a sunbow laughs and is lost on the waves that range
And reck not of light that flickers or spray that flies.
But the sun withdraws not, the woodland shrinks not or sighs,
No sweet thing sickens with sense or with fear of change;
Light wounds not, darkness blinds not, my steadfast eyes.

Only the soul in my sense that receives the soul
Whence now my spirit is kindled with breathless bliss
Knows well if the light that wounds it with love makes whole,
If hopes that carol be louder than fears that hiss,
If truth be spoken of flowers and of waves that kiss,
Of clouds and stars that contend for a sunbright goal.
And yet may I dream that I dream not indeed of this?

An earth-born dreamer, constrained by the bonds of birth,
Held fast by the flesh, compelled by his veins that beat
And kindle to rapture or wrath, to desire or to mirth,
May hear not surely the fall of immortal feet,
May feel not surely if heaven upon earth be sweet;
And here is my sense fulfilled of the joys of earth,

Light, silence, bloom, shade, murmur of leaves that meet.

Bloom, fervour, and perfume of grasses and flowers aglow,
Breathe and brighten about me: the darkness gleams,
The sweet light shivers and laughs on the slopes below,
Made soft by leaves that lighten and change like dreams;
The silence thrills with the whisper of secret streams
That well from the heart of the woodland: these I know:
Earth bore them, heaven sustained them with showers and beams.

I lean my face to the heather, and drink the sun
Whose flame-lit odour satiates the flowers: mine eyes
Close, and the goal of delight and of life is one:
No more I crave of earth or her kindred skies.
No more? But the joy that springs from them smiles and flies:
The sweet work wrought of them surely, the good work done,
If the mind and the face of the season be loveless, dies.

Thee, therefore, thee would I come to, cleave to, cling,
If haply thy heart be kind and thy gifts be good,
Unknown sweet spirit, whose vesture is soft in spring,
In summer splendid, in autumn pale as the wood
That shudders and wanes and shrinks as a shamed thing should,
In winter bright as the mail of a war-worn king
Who stands where foes fled far from the face of him stood.

My spirit or thine is it, breath of thy life or of mine,
Which fills my sense with a rapture that casts out fear?
Pan's dim frown wanes, and his wild eyes brighten as thine,
Transformed as night or as day by the kindling year.
Earth-born, or mine eye were withered that sees, mine ear
That hears were stricken to death by the sense divine,
Earth-born I know thee: but heaven is about me here.

The terror that whispers in darkness and flames in light,
The doubt that speaks in the silence of earth and sea,
The sense, more fearful at noon than in midmost night,
Of wrath scarce hushed and of imminent ill to be,
Where are they? Heaven is as earth, and as heaven to me
Earth: for the shadows that sundered them here take flight;
And nought is all, as am I, but a dream of thee.

ON THE SOUTH COAST

TO THEODORE WATTS

Hills and valleys where April rallies his radiant squadron of flowers and birds,
Steep strange beaches and lustrous reaches of fluctuant sea that the land engirds,
Fields and downs that the sunrise crowns with life diviner than lives in words,

Day by day of resurgent May salute the sun with sublime acclaim,
Change and brighten with hours that lighten and darken, girdled with cloud or flame;
Earth's fair face in alternate grace beams, blooms, and lowers, and is yet the same.

Twice each day the divine sea's play makes glad with glory that comes and goes
Field and street that her waves keep sweet, when past the bounds of their old repose,
Fast and fierce in renewed reverse, the foam-flecked estuary ebbs and flows.

Broad and bold through the stays of old staked fast with trunks of the wildwood tree,
Up from shoreward, impelled far forward, by marsh and meadow, by lawn and lea,
Inland still at her own wild will swells, rolls, and revels the surging sea.

Strong as time, and as faith sublime,—clothed round with shadows of hopes and fears,
Nights and morrows, and joys and sorrows, alive with passion of prayers and tears,—
Stands the shrine that has seen decline eight hundred waxing and waning years.

Tower set square to the storms of air and change of season that glooms and glows,
Wall and roof of it tempest-proof, and equal ever to suns and snows,
Bright with riches of radiant niches and pillars smooth as a straight stem grows.

Aisle and nave that the whelming wave of time has whelmed not or touched or neared,
Arch and vault without stain or fault, by hands of craftsmen we know not reared,
Time beheld them, and time was quelled; and change passed by them as one that feared.

Time that flies as a dream, and dies as dreams that die with the sleep they feed,
Here alone in a garb of stone incarnate stands as a god indeed,
Stern and fair, and of strength to bear all burdens mortal to man's frail seed.

Men and years are as leaves or tears that storm or sorrow is fain to shed:
These go by as the winds that sigh, and none takes note of them quick or dead:
Time, whose breath is their birth and death, folds here his pinions, and bows his head.

Still the sun that beheld begun the work wrought here of unwearied hands
Sees, as then, though the Red King's men held ruthless rule over lawless lands,
Stand their massive design, impassive, pure and proud as a virgin stands.

Statelier still as the years fulfil their count, subserving her sacred state,
Grows the hoary grey church whose story silence utters and age makes great:
Statelier seems it than shines in dreams the face unveiled of unvanquished fate.

Fate, more high than the star-shown sky, more deep than waters unsounded, shines
Keen and far as the final star on souls that seek not for charms or signs;
Yet more bright is the love-shown light of men's hands lighted in songs or shrines.

Love and trust that the grave's deep dust can soil not, neither may fear put out,
Witness yet that their record set stands fast, though years be as hosts in rout,
Spent and slain; but the signs remain that beat back darkness and cast forth doubt.

Men that wrought by the grace of thought and toil things goodlier than praise dare trace,
Fair as all that the world may call most fair, save only the sea's own face,
Shrines or songs that the world's change wrongs not, live by grace of their own gift's grace.

Dead, their names that the night reclaims—alive, their works that the day relumes—
Sink and stand, as in stone and sand engraven: none may behold their tombs:
Nights and days shall record their praise while here this flower of their grafting blooms.

Flower more fair than the sun-thrilled air bids laugh and lighten and wax and rise,
Fruit more bright than the fervent light sustains with strength from the kindled skies,
Flower and fruit that the deathless root of man's love rears though the man's name dies.

Stately stands it, the work of hands unknown of: statelier, afar and near,
Rise around it the heights that bound our landward gaze from the seaboard here;
Downs that swerve and aspire, in curve and change of heights that the dawn holds dear.

Dawn falls fair on the grey walls there confronting dawn, on the low green lea,
Lone and sweet as for fairies' feet held sacred, silent and strange and free,
Wild and wet with its rills; but yet more fair falls dawn on the fairer sea.

Eastward, round by the high green bound of hills that fold the remote fields in,
Strive and shine on the low sea-line fleet waves and beams when the days begin;
Westward glow, when the days burn low, the sun that yields and the stars that win.

Rose-red eve on the seas that heave sinks fair as dawn when the first ray peers;
Winds are glancing from sunbright Lancing to Shoreham, crowned with the grace of years;
Shoreham, clad with the sunset, glad and grave with glory that death reveres.

Death, more proud than the kings' heads bowed before him, stronger than all things, bows
Here his head: as if death were dead, and kingship plucked from his crownless brows,
Life hath here such a face of cheer as change appals not and time avows.

Skies fulfilled with the sundown, stilled and splendid, spread as a flower that spreads,
Pave with rarer device and fairer than heaven's the luminous oyster-beds,
Grass-embanked, and in square plots ranked, inlaid with gems that the sundown sheds.

Squares more bright and with lovelier light than heaven that kindled it shines with shine
Warm and soft as the dome aloft, but heavenlier yet than the sun's own shrine:
Heaven is high, but the water-sky lit here seems deeper and more divine.

Flowers on flowers, that the whole world's bowers may show not, here may the sunset show,
Lightly graven in the waters paven with ghostly gold by the clouds aglow:
Bright as love is the vault above, but lovelier lightens the wave below.

Rosy grey, or as fiery spray full-plumed, or greener than emerald, gleams
Plot by plot as the skies allot for each its glory, divine as dreams
Lit with fire of appeased desire which sounds the secret of all that seems;

Dreams that show what we fain would know, and know not save by the grace of sleep,
Sleep whose hands have removed the bands that eyes long waking and fain to weep
Feel fast bound on them—light around them strange, and darkness above them steep.

Yet no vision that heals division of love from love, and renews awhile
Life and breath in the lips where death has quenched the spirit of speech and smile,
Shows on earth, or in heaven's mid mirth, where no fears enter or doubts defile,

Aught more fair than the radiant air and water here by the twilight wed,
Here made one by the waning sun whose last love quickens to rosebright red
Half the crown of the soft high down that rears to northward its wood-girt head.

There, when day is at height of sway, men's eyes who stand, as we oft have stood,
High where towers with its world of flowers the golden spinny that flanks the wood,
See before and around them shore and seaboard glad as their gifts are good.

Higher and higher to the north aspire the green smooth-swelling unending downs;
East and west on the brave earth's breast glow girdle-jewels of gleaming towns;
Southward shining, the lands declining subside in peace that the sea's light crowns.

Westward wide in its fruitful pride the plain lies lordly with plenteous grace;
Fair as dawn's when the fields and lawns desire her glitters the glad land's face:
Eastward yet is the sole sign set of elder days and a lordlier race.

Down beneath us afar, where seethe in wilder weather the tides aflow,
Hurled up hither and drawn down thither in quest of rest that they may not know,
Still as dew on a flower the blue broad stream now sleeps in the fields below.

Mild and bland in the fair green land it smiles, and takes to its heart the sky;
Scarce the meads and the fens, the reeds and grasses, still as they stand or lie,
Wear the palm of a statelier calm than rests on waters that pass them by.

Yet shall these, when the winds and seas of equal days and coequal nights
Rage, rejoice, and uplift a voice whose sound is even as a sword that smites,
Felt and heard as a doomsman's word from seaward reaches to landward heights,

Lift their heart up, and take their part of triumph, swollen and strong with rage,
Rage elate with desire and great with pride that tempest and storm assuage;
So their chime in the ear of time has rung from age to rekindled age.

Fair and dear is the land's face here, and fair man's work as a man's may be:
Dear and fair as the sunbright air is here the record that speaks him free;
Free by birth of a sacred earth, and regent ever of all the sea.

AN AUTUMN VISION

OCTOBER 31, 1889

I

Is it Midsummer here in the heavens that illumine October on earth?
Can the year, when his heart is fulfilled with desire of the days of his mirth,
Redeem them, recall, or remember?
For a memory recalling the rapture of earth, and redeeming the sky,
Shines down from the heights to the depths: will the watchword of dawn be July
When to-morrow acclaims November?
The stern salutation of sorrow to death or repentance to shame
Was all that the season was wont to accord her of grace or acclaim;
No lightnings of love and of laughter.
But here, in the laugh of the loud west wind from around and above,
In the flash of the waters beneath him, what sound or what light but of love
Rings round him or leaps forth after?

II

Wind beloved of earth and sky and sea beyond all winds that blow,
Wind whose might in fight was England's on her mightiest warrior day,
South-west wind, whose breath for her was life, and fire to scourge her foe,
Steel to smite and death to drive him down an unreturning way,
Well-beloved and welcome, sounding all the clarions of the sky,
Rolling all the marshalled waters toward the charge that storms the shore,
We receive, acclaim, salute thee, we who live and dream and die,
As the mightiest mouth of song that ever spake acclaimed of yore.
We that live as they that perish praise thee, lord of cloud and wave,
Wind of winds, clothed on with darkness whence as lightning light comes forth,
We that know thee strong to guard and smite, to scatter and to save,
We to whom the south-west wind is dear as Athens held the north.
He for her waged war as thou for us against all powers defiant,
Fleets full-fraught with storm from Persia, laden deep with death from Spain:
Thee the giant god of song and battle hailed as god and giant,
Yet not his but ours the land is whence thy praise should ring and rain;
Rain as rapture shed from song, and ring as trumpets blown for battle,
Sound and sing before thee, loud and glad as leaps and sinks the sea:
Yea, the sea's white steeds are curbed and spurred of thee, and pent as cattle,
Yet they laugh with love and pride to live, subdued not save of thee.
Ears that hear thee hear in heaven the sound of widening wings gigantic,
Eyes that see the cloud-lift westward see thy darkening brows divine;
Wings whose measure is the limit of the limitless Atlantic,
Brows that bend, and bid the sovereign sea submit her soul to thine.

III

Twelve days since is it—twelve days gone,
Lord of storm, that a storm-bow shone
Higher than sweeps thy sublime dark wing,
Fair as dawn is and sweet like spring?

Never dawn in the deep wide east
Spread so splendid and strange a feast,
Whence the soul as it drank and fed
Felt such rapture of wonder shed.

Never spring in the wild wood's heart
Felt such flowers at her footfall start,
Born of earth, as arose on sight
Born of heaven and of storm and light.

Stern and sullen, the grey grim sea
Swelled and strove as in toils, though free,
Free as heaven, and as heaven sublime,
Clear as heaven of the toils of time.

IV

Suddenly, sheer from the heights to the depths of the sky and the sea,
Sprang from the darkness alive as a vision of life to be
Glory triune and transcendent of colour afar and afire,
Arching and darkening the darkness with light as of dream or desire.
Heaven, in the depth of its height, shone wistful and wan from above:
Earth from beneath, and the sea, shone stricken and breathless with love.
As a shadow may shine, so shone they; as ghosts of the viewless blest,
That sleep hath sight of alive in a rapture of sunbright rest,
The green earth glowed and the grey sky gleamed for a wondrous while;
And the storm's full frown was crossed by the light of its own deep smile.
As the darkness of thought and of passion is touched by the light that gives
Life deathless as love from the depth of a spirit that sees and lives,
From the soul of a seer and a singer, wherein as a scroll unfurled
Lies open the scripture of light and of darkness, the word of the world,
So, shapeless and measureless, lurid as anguish and haggard as crime,
Pale as the front of oblivion and dark as the heart of time,
The wild wan heaven at its height was assailed and subdued and made
More fair than the skies that know not of storm and endure not shade.
The grim sea-swell, grey, sleepless, and sad as a soul estranged,
Shone, smiled, took heart, and was glad of its wrath: and the world's face changed.

V

Up from moorlands northward gleaming
Even to heaven's transcendent height,
Clothed with massive cloud, and seeming
All one fortress reared of night,
Down to where the deep sea, dreaming
Angry dreams, lay dark and white,
White as death and dark as fate,
Heaving with the strong wind's weight,
Sad with stormy pride of state,
One full rainbow shone elate.

Up from inmost memory's dwelling
Where the light of life abides,
Where the past finds tongue, foretelling
Time that comes and grace that guides,
Power that saves and sways, compelling
Souls that ebb and flow like tides,
Shone or seemed to shine and swim
Through the cloud-surf great and grim,
Thought's live surge, the soul of him
By whose light the sun looks dim.

In what synod were they sitting,
All the gods and lords of time,
Whence they watched as fen-fires flitting
Years and names of men sublime,
When their counsels found it fitting
One should stand where none might climb—
None of man begotten, none
Born of men beneath the sun
Till the race of time be run,
Save this heaven-enfranchised one?

With what rapture of creation
Was the soul supernal thrilled,
With what pride of adoration
Was the world's heart fired and filled,
Heaved in heavenward exaltation
Higher than hopes or dreams might build,
Grave with awe not known while he
Was not, mad with glorious glee
As the sun-saluted sea,
When his hour bade Shakespeare be?

There, clear as night beholds her crowning seven,
The sea beheld his likeness set in heaven.
The shadow of his spirit full in sight
Shone: for the shadow of that soul is light.
Nor heaven alone bore witness: earth avowed
Him present, and acclaimed of storm aloud.
From the arching sky to the ageless hills and sea
The whole world, visible, audible, was he:
Each part of all that wove that wondrous whole
The raiment of the presence of his soul.
The sun that smote and kissed the dark to death
Spake, smiled, and strove, like song's triumphant breath;
The soundless cloud whose thunderous heart was dumb
Swelled, lowered, and shrank to feel its conqueror come.
Yet high from heaven its empire vast and vain
Frowned, and renounced not night's reluctant reign.
The serpentine swift sounds and shapes wherein
The stainless sea mocks earth and death and sin,
Crawls dark as craft, or flashes keen as hate,
Subdued and insubmissive, strong like fate
And weak like man, bore wrathful witness yet
That storms and sins are more than suns that set;
That evil everlasting, girt for strife
Eternal, wars with hope as death with life.
The dark sharp shifting wind that bade the waves
Falter, lose heart, bow down like foes made slaves,
And waxed within more bitter as they bowed,
Baffling the sea, swallowing the sun with cloud,
Devouring fast as fire on earth devours
And hungering hard as frost that feeds on flowers,
Clothed round with fog that reeked as fume from hell,
And darkening with its miscreative spell
Light, glad and keen and splendid as the sword
Whose heft had known Othello's hand its lord,
Spake all the soul that hell drew back to greet
And felt its fire shrink shuddering from his feet.
Far off the darkness darkened, and recoiled,
And neared again, and triumphed: and the coiled
Colourless cloud and sea discoloured grew
Conscious of horror huge as heaven, and knew
Where Goneril's soul made chill and foul the mist,
And all the leprous life in Regan hissed.
Fierce homeless ghosts, rejected of the pit,
From hell to hell of storm fear watched them flit.
About them and before, the dull grey gloom
Shuddered, and heaven seemed hateful as the tomb

That shrinks from resurrection; and from out
That sullen hell which girt their shades about
The nether soul that lurks and lowers within
Man, made of dust and fire and shame and sin,
Breathed: all the cloud that felt it breathe and blight
Was blue as plague or black as thunderous night.
Elect of hell, the children of his hate
Thronged, as to storm sweet heaven's triumphal gate.
The terror of his giving rose and shone
Imminent: life had put its likeness on.
But higher than all its horrent height of shade
Shone sovereign, seen by light itself had made,
Above the woes of all the world, above
Life, sin, and death, his myriad-minded love.
From landward heights whereon the radiance leant
Full-fraught from heaven, intense and imminent,
To depths wherein the seething strengths of cloud
Scarce matched the wrath of waves whereon they bowed,
From homeborn pride and kindling love of home
To the outer skies and seas of fire and foam,
From splendour soft as dew that sundawn thrills
To gloom that shudders round the world it fills,
From midnights murmuring round Titania's ear
To midnights maddening round the rage of Lear,
The wonder woven of storm and sun became
One with the light that lightens from his name.
The music moving on the sea that felt
The storm-wind even as snows of springtide melt
Was blithe as Ariel's hand or voice might make
And bid all grief die gladly for its sake.
And there the soul alive in ear and eye
That watched the wonders of an hour pass by
Saw brighter than all stars that heaven inspheres
The silent splendour of Cordelia's tears,
Felt in the whispers of the quickening wind
The radiance of the laugh of Rosalind,
And heard, in sounds that melt the souls of men
With love of love, the tune of Imogen.

VII

For the strong north-east is not strong to subdue and to slay the divine south-west,
And the darkness is less than the light that it darkens, and dies in reluctant rest.
It hovers and hangs on the labouring and trembling ascent of the dawn from the deep,
Till the sun's eye quicken the world and the waters, and smite it again into sleep.
Night, holy and starry, the fostress of souls, with the fragrance of heaven in her breath,
Subdues with the sense of her godhead the forces and mysteries of sorrow and death.

Eternal as dawn's is the comfort she gives: but the mist that beleaguers and slays
Comes, passes, and is not: the strength of it withers, appalled or assuaged by the day's.
Faith, haggard as Fear that had borne her, and dark as the sire that begat her, Despair,
Held rule on the soul of the world and the song of it saddening through ages that were;
Dim centuries that darkened and brightened and darkened again, and the soul of their song
Was great as their grief, and sublime as their suffering, and strong as their sorrows were strong.
It knew not, it saw not, but shadows triune, and evoked by the strength of their spell
Dark hell, and the mountain of anguish, and heaven that was hollower and harder than hell.
These are not: the womb of the darkness that bare them rejects them, and knows them no more:
Thought, fettered in misery and iron, revives in the light that it lived in of yore.
For the soul that is wisdom and freedom, the spirit of England redeemed from her past,
Speaks life through the lips of the master and lord of her children, the first and the last.
Thought, touched by his hand and redeemed by his breath, sees, hears, and accepts from above
The limitless lightnings of vision and passion, the measureless music of love.

A SWIMMER'S DREAM

NOVEMBER 4, 1889

I

Dawn is dim on the dark soft water,
Soft and passionate, dark and sweet.
Love's own self was the deep sea's daughter,
Fair and flawless from face to feet,
Hailed of all when the world was golden,
Loved of lovers whose names beholden
Thrill men's eyes as with light of olden
Days more glad than their flight was fleet.

So they sang: but for men that love her,
Souls that hear not her word in vain,
Earth beside her and heaven above her
Seem but shadows that wax and wane.
Softer than sleep's are the sea's caresses,
Kinder than love's that betrays and blesses,
Blither than spring's when her flowerful tresses
Shake forth sunlight and shine with rain.

All the strength of the waves that perish
Swells beneath me and laughs and sighs,
Sighs for love of the life they cherish,
Laughs to know that it lives and dies,
Dies for joy of its life, and lives
Thrilled with joy that its brief death gives—
Death whose laugh or whose breath forgives

Change that bids it subside and rise.

II

Hard and heavy, remote but nearing,
Sunless hangs the severe sky's weight,
Cloud on cloud, though the wind be veering
Heaped on high to the sundawn's gate.
Dawn and even and noon are one,
Veiled with vapour and void of sun;
Nought in sight or in fancied hearing
Now less mighty than time or fate.

The grey sky gleams and the grey seas glimmer,
Pale and sweet as a dream's delight,
As a dream's where darkness and light seem dimmer,
Touched by dawn or subdued by night.
The dark wind, stern and sublime and sad,
Swings the rollers to westward, clad
With lustrous shadow that lures the swimmer,
Lures and lulls him with dreams of light.

Light, and sleep, and delight, and wonder,
Change, and rest, and a charm of cloud,
Fill the world of the skies whereunder
Heaves and quivers and pants aloud
All the world of the waters, hoary
Now, but clothed with its own live glory,
That mates the lightning and mocks the thunder
With light more living and word more proud.

III

Far off westward, whither sets the sounding strife,
Strife more sweet than peace, of shoreless waves whose glee
Scorns the shore and loves the wind that leaves them free,
Strange as sleep and pale as death and fair as life,
Shifts the moonlight-coloured sunshine on the sea.

Toward the sunset's goal the sunless waters crowd,
Fast as autumn days toward winter: yet it seems
Here that autumn wanes not, here that woods and streams
Lose not heart and change not likeness, chilled and bowed,
Warped and wrinkled: here the days are fair as dreams.

IV

O russet-robed November,
What ails thee so to smile?
Chill August, pale September,
Endured a woful while,
And fell as falls an ember
From forth a flameless pile:
But golden-girt November
Bids all she looks on smile.

The lustrous foliage, waning
As wanes the morning moon,
Here falling, here refraining,
Outbraves the pride of June
With statelier semblance, feigning
No fear lest death be soon:
As though the woods thus waning
Should wax to meet the moon.

As though, when fields lie stricken
By grey December's breath,
These lordlier growths that sicken
And die for fear of death
Should feel the sense requicken
That hears what springtide saith
And thrills for love, spring-stricken
And pierced with April's breath.

The keen white-winged north-easter
That stings and spurs thy sea
Doth yet but feed and feast her
With glowing sense of glee:
Calm chained her, storm released her,
And storm's glad voice was he:
South-wester or north-easter,
Thy winds rejoice the sea.

V

A dream, a dream is it all—the season,
The sky, the water, the wind, the shore?
A day-born dream of divine unreason,
A marvel moulded of sleep—no more?
For the cloudlike wave that my limbs while cleaving
Feel as in slumber beneath them heaving
Soothes the sense as to slumber, leaving

Sense of nought that was known of yore.

A purer passion, a lordlier leisure,
A peace more happy than lives on land,
Fulfils with pulse of diviner pleasure
The dreaming head and the steering hand.
I lean my cheek to the cold grey pillow,
The deep soft swell of the full broad billow,
And close mine eyes for delight past measure,
And wish the wheel of the world would stand.

The wild-winged hour that we fain would capture
Falls as from heaven that its light feet clomb,
So brief, so soft, and so full the rapture
Was felt that soothed me with sense of home.
To sleep, to swim, and to dream, for ever—
Such joy the vision of man saw never;
For here too soon will a dark day sever
The sea-bird's wing from the sea-wave's foam.

A dream, and more than a dream, and dimmer
At once and brighter than dreams that flee,
The moment's joy of the seaward swimmer
Abides, remembered as truth may be.
Not all the joy and not all the glory
Must fade as leaves when the woods wax hoary;
For there the downs and the sea-banks glimmer,
And here to south of them swells the sea.

GRACE DARLING

Take, O star of all our seas, from not an alien hand,
Homage paid of song bowed down before thy glory's face,
Thou the living light of all our lovely stormy strand,
Thou the brave north-country's very glory of glories, Grace.

Loud and dark about the lighthouse rings and glares the night;
Glares with foam-lit gloom and darkling fire of storm and spray,
Rings with roar of winds in chase and rage of waves in flight,
Howls and hisses as with mouths of snakes and wolves at bay.
Scarce the cliffs of the islets, scarce the walls of Joyous Gard,
Flash to sight between the deadlier lightnings of the sea:
Storm is lord and master of a midnight evil-starred,
Nor may sight or fear discern what evil stars may be.
Dark as death and white as snow the sea-swell scowls and shines,
Heaves and yearns and pants for prey, from ravening lip to lip,

Strong in rage of rapturous anguish, lines on hurtling lines,
Ranks on charging ranks, that break and rend the battling ship.
All the night is mad and murderous: who shall front the night?
Not the prow that labours, helpless as a storm-blown leaf,
Where the rocks and waters, darkling depth and beetling height,
Rage with wave on shattering wave and thundering reef on reef.
Death is fallen upon the prisoners there of darkness, bound
Like as thralls with links of iron fast in bonds of doom;
How shall any way to break the bands of death be found,
Any hand avail to pluck them from that raging tomb?
All the night is great with child of death: no stars above
Show them hope in heaven, no lights from shores ward help on earth.
Is there help or hope to seaward, is there help in love,
Hope in pity, where the ravening hounds of storm make mirth?
Where the light but shows the naked eyeless face of Death
Nearer, laughing dumb and grim across the loud live storm?
Not in human heart or hand or speech of human breath,
Surely, nor in saviours found of mortal face or form.
Yet below the light, between the reefs, a skiff shot out
Seems a sea-bird fain to breast and brave the strait fierce pass
Whence the channelled roar of waters driven in raging rout,
Pent and pressed and maddened, speaks their monstrous might and mass.
Thunder heaves and howls about them, lightning leaps and flashes,
Hard at hand, not high in heaven, but close between the walls
Heaped and hollowed of the storms of old, whence reels and crashes
All the rage of all the unbaffled wave that breaks and falls.
Who shall thwart the madness and the gladness of it, laden
Full with heavy fate, and joyous as the birds that whirl?
Nought in heaven or earth, if not one mortal-moulded maiden,
Nought if not the soul that glorifies a northland girl.
Not the rocks that break may baffle, not the reefs that thwart
Stay the ravenous rapture of the waves that crowd and leap;
Scarce their flashing laughter shows the hunger of their heart,
Scarce their lion-throated roar the wrath at heart they keep.
Child and man and woman in the grasp of death clenched fast
Tremble, clothed with darkness round about, and scarce draw breath,
Scarce lift eyes up toward the light that saves not, scarce may cast
Thought or prayer up, caught and trammelled in the snare of death.
Not as sea-mews cling and laugh or sun their plumes and sleep
Cling and cower the wild night's waifs of shipwreck, blind with fear,
Where the fierce reef scarce yields foothold that a bird might keep,
And the clamorous darkness deadens eye and deafens ear.
Yet beyond their helpless hearing, out of hopeless sight,
Saviours, armed and girt upon with strength of heart, fare forth,
Sire and daughter, hand on oar and face against the night,
Maid and man whose names are beacons ever to the North.
Nearer now; but all the madness of the storming surf
Hounds and roars them back; but roars and hounds them back in vain:

As a pleasure-skiff may graze the lake-embanking turf,
So the boat that bears them grates the rock where-toward they strain.
Dawn as fierce and haggard as the face of night scarce guides
Toward the cries that rent and clove the darkness, crying for aid,
Hours on hours, across the engorged reluctance of the tides,
Sire and daughter, high-souled man and mightier-hearted maid.
Not the bravest land that ever breasted war's grim sea,
Hurled her foes back harried on the lowlands whence they came,
Held her own and smote her smiters down, while such durst be,
Shining northward, shining southward, as the aurorean flame,
Not our mother, not Northumberland, brought ever forth,
Though no southern shore may match the sons that kiss her mouth,
Children worthier all the birthright given of the ardent north
Where the fire of hearts outburns the suns that fire the south.
Even such fire was this that lit them, not from lowering skies
Where the darkling dawn flagged, stricken in the sun's own shrine,
Down the gulf of storm subsiding, till their earnest eyes
Find the relics of the ravening night that spared but nine.
Life by life the man redeems them, head by storm-worn head,
While the girl's hand stays the boat whereof the waves are fain:
Ah, but woe for one, the mother clasping fast her dead!
Happier, had the surges slain her with her children slain.
Back they bear, and bring between them safe the woful nine,
Where above the ravenous Hawkers fixed at watch for prey
Storm and calm behold the Longstone's towering signal shine
Now as when that labouring night brought forth a shuddering day.
Now as then, though like the hounds of storm against her snarling
All the clamorous years between us storm down many a fame,
As our sires beheld before us we behold Grace Darling
Crowned and throned our queen, and as they hailed we hail her name.
Nay, not ours alone, her kinsfolk born, though chiefliest ours,
East and west and south acclaim her queen of England's maids,
Star more sweet than all their stars and flower than all their flowers,
Higher in heaven and earth than star that sets or flower that fades.
How should land or sea that nurtured her forget, or love
Hold not fast her fame for us while aught is borne in mind?
Land and sea beneath us, sun and moon and stars above,
Bear the bright soul witness, seen of all but souls born blind.
Stars and moon and sun may wax and wane, subside and rise,
Age on age as flake on flake of showering snows be shed:
Not till earth be sunless, not till death strike blind the skies,
May the deathless love that waits on deathless deeds be dead.

Years on years have withered since beside the hearth once thine
I, too young to have seen thee, touched thy father's hallowed hand:
Thee and him shall all men see for ever, stars that shine
While the sea that spared thee girds and glorifies the land.

LOCH TORRIDON

TO E. H.

The dawn of night more fair than morning rose,
Stars hurrying forth on stars, as snows on snows
Haste when the wind and winter bid them speed.
Vague miles of moorland road behind us lay
Scarce traversed ere the day
Sank, and the sun forsook us at our need,
Belated. Where we thought to have rested, rest
Was none; for soft Maree's dim quivering breast,
Bound round with gracious inland girth of green
And fearless of the wild wave-wandering West,
Shone shelterless for strangers; and unseen
The goal before us lay
Of all our blithe and strange and strenuous day.

For when the northering road faced westward—when
The dark sharp sudden gorge dropped seaward—then,
Beneath the stars, between the steeps, the track
We followed, lighted not of moon or sun,
And plunging whither none
Might guess, while heaven and earth were hoar and black,
Seemed even the dim still pass whence none turns back:
And through the twilight leftward of the way,
And down the dark, with many a laugh and leap,
The light blithe hill-streams shone from scaur to steep
In glittering pride of play;
And ever while the night grew great and deep
We felt but saw not what the hills would keep
Sacred awhile from sense of moon or star;
And full and far
Beneath us, sweet and strange as heaven may be,
The sea.

The very sea: no mountain-moulded lake
Whose fluctuant shapeliness is fain to take
Shape from the steadfast shore that rules it round,
And only from the storms a casual sound:
The sea, that harbours in her heart sublime
The supreme heart of music deep as time,
And in her spirit strong
The spirit of all imaginable song.

Not a whisper or lisp from the waters: the skies were not silenter. Peace

Was between them; a passionless rapture of respite as soft as release.
Not a sound, but a sense that possessed and pervaded with patient delight
The soul and the body, clothed round with the comfort of limitless night.
Night infinite, living, adorable, loved of the land and the sea:
Night, mother of mercies, who saith to the spirits in prison, Be free.
And softer than dewfall, and kindlier than starlight, and keener than wine,
Came round us the fragrance of waters, the life of the breath of the brine.
We saw not, we heard not, the face or the voice of the waters: we knew
By the darkling delight of the wind as the sense of the sea in it grew,
By the pulse of the darkness about us enkindled and quickened, that here,
Unseen and unheard of us, surely the goal we had faith in was near.
A silence diviner than music, a darkness diviner than light,
Fulfilled as from heaven with a measureless comfort the measure of night.

But never a roof for shelter
And never a sign for guide
Rose doubtful or visible: only
And hardly and gladly we heard
The soft waves whisper and welter,
Subdued, and allured to subside,
By the mild night's magic: the lonely
Sweet silence was soothed, not stirred,
By the noiseless noise of the gleaming
Glad ripples, that played and sighed,
Kissed, laughed, recoiled, and relented,
Whispered, flickered, and fled.
No season was this for dreaming
How oft, with a stormier tide,
Had the wrath of the winds been vented
On sons of the tribes long dead:
The tribes whom time, and the changes
Of things, and the stress of doom,
Have erased and effaced; forgotten
As wrecks or weeds of the shore
In sight of the stern hill-ranges
That hardly may change their gloom
When the fruits of the years wax rotten
And the seed of them springs no more.
For the dim strait footway dividing
The waters that breathed below
Led safe to the kindliest of shelters
That ever awoke into light:
And still in remembrance abiding
Broods over the stars that glow
And the water that eddies and welters
The passionate peace of the night.

All night long, in the world of sleep,

Skies and waters were soft and deep:
Shadow clothed them, and silence made
Soundless music of dream and shade:
All above us, the livelong night,
Shadow, kindled with sense of light;
All around us, the brief night long,
Silence, laden with sense of song.
Stars and mountains without, we knew,
Watched and waited, the soft night through:
All unseen, but divined and dear,
Thrilled the touch of the sea's breath near:
All unheard, but alive like sound,
Throbbed the sense of the sea's life round:
Round us, near us, in depth and height,
Soft as darkness and keen as light.

And the dawn leapt in at my casement: and there, as I rose, at my feet
No waves of the landlocked waters, no lake submissive and sweet,
Soft slave of the lordly seasons, whose breath may loose it or freeze;
But to left and to right and ahead was the ripple whose pulse is the sea's.
From the gorge we had travelled by starlight the sunrise, winged and aflame,
Shone large on the live wide wavelets that shuddered with joy as it came;
As it came and caressed and possessed them, till panting and laughing with light
From mountain to mountain the water was kindled and stung to delight.
And the grey gaunt heights that embraced and constrained and compelled it were glad,
And the rampart of rock, stark naked, that thwarted and barred it, was clad
With a stern grey splendour of sunrise: and scarce had I sprung to the sea
When the dawn and the water were wedded, the hills and the sky set free.
The chain of the night was broken: the waves that embraced me and smiled
And flickered and fawned in the sunlight, alive, unafraid, undefiled,
Were sweeter to swim in than air, though fulfilled with the mounting morn,
Could be for the birds whose triumph rejoiced that a day was born.

And a day was arisen indeed for us. Years and the changes of years
Clothed round with their joys and their sorrows, and dead as their hopes and their fears,
Lie noteless and nameless, unlit by remembrance or record of days
Worth wonder or memory, or cursing or blessing, or passion or praise,
Between us who live and forget not, but yearn with delight in it yet,
And the day we forget not, and never may live and may think to forget.
And the years that were kindlier and fairer, and kindled with pleasures as keen,
Have eclipsed not with lights or with shadows the light on the face of it seen.
For softly and surely, as nearer the boat that we gazed from drew,
The face of the precipice opened and bade us as birds pass through,
And the bark shot sheer to the sea through the strait of the sharp steep cleft,
The portal that opens with imminent rampires to right and to left,
Sublime as the sky they darken and strange as a spell-struck dream,
On the world unconfined of the mountains, the reign of the sea supreme,
The kingdom of westward waters, wherein when we swam we knew

The waves that we clove were boundless, the wind on our brows that blew
Had swept no land and no lake, and had warred not on tower or on tree,
But came on us hard out of heaven, and alive with the soul of the sea.

THE PALACE OF PAN

INSCRIBED TO MY MOTHER

September, all glorious with gold, as a king
In the radiance of triumph attired,
Outlightening the summer, outsweetening the spring,
Broods wide on the woodlands with limitless wing,
A presence of all men desired.

Far eastward and westward the sun-coloured lands
Smile warm as the light on them smiles;
And statelier than temples upbuilded with hands,
Tall column by column, the sanctuary stands
Of the pine-forest's infinite aisles.

Mute worship, too fervent for praise or for prayer,
Possesses the spirit with peace,
Fulfilled with the breath of the luminous air,
The fragrance, the silence, the shadows as fair
As the rays that recede or increase.

Ridged pillars that redden aloft and aloof,
With never a branch for a nest,
Sustain the sublime indivisible roof,
To the storm and the sun in his majesty proof,
And awful as waters at rest.

Man's hand hath not measured the height of them; thought
May measure not, awe may not know;
In its shadow the woofs of the woodland are wrought;
As a bird is the sun in the toils of them caught,
And the flakes of it scattered as snow.

As the shreds of a plumage of gold on the ground
The sun-flakes by multitudes lie,
Shed loose as the petals of roses discrowned
On the floors of the forest engilt and embrowned
And reddened afar and anigh.

Dim centuries with darkling inscrutable hands
Have reared and secluded the shrine

For gods that we know not, and kindled as brands
On the altar the years that are dust, and their sands
Time's glass has forgotten for sign.

A temple whose transepts are measured by miles,
Whose chancel has morning for priest,
Whose floor-work the foot of no spoiler defiles,
Whose musical silence no music beguiles,
No festivals limit its feast.

The noon's ministration, the night's and the dawn's,
Conceals not, reveals not for man,
On the slopes of the herbless and blossomless lawns,
Some track of a nymph's or some trail of a faun's
To the place of the slumber of Pan.

Thought, kindled and quickened by worship and wonder
To rapture too sacred for fear
On the ways that unite or divide them in sunder,
Alone may discern if about them or under
Be token or trace of him here.

With passionate awe that is deeper than panic
The spirit subdued and unshaken
Takes heed of the godhead terrene and Titanic
Whose footfall is felt on the breach of volcanic
Sharp steeps that their fire has forsaken.

By a spell more serene than the dim necromantic
Dead charms of the past and the night,
Or the terror that lurked in the noon to make frantic
Where Etna takes shape from the limbs of gigantic
Dead gods disanointed of might,

The spirit made one with the spirit whose breath
Makes noon in the woodland sublime
Abides as entranced in a presence that saith
Things loftier than life and serener than death,
Triumphant and silent as time.

PINE RIDGE: September 1893

A YEAR'S CAROLS

JANUARY

Hail, January, that bearest here
On snowbright breasts the babe-faced year
That weeps and trembles to be born.
Hail, maid and mother, strong and bright,
Hooded and cloaked and shod with white,
Whose eyes are stars that match the morn.
Thy forehead braves the storm's bent bow,
Thy feet enkindle stars of snow.

FEBRUARY

Wan February with weeping cheer,
Whose cold hand guides the youngling year
Down misty roads of mire and rime,
Before thy pale and fitful face
The shrill wind shifts the clouds apace
Through skies the morning scarce may climb.
Thine eyes are thick with heavy tears,
But lit with hopes that light the year's.

MARCH

Hail, happy March, whose foot on earth
Rings as the blast of martial mirth
When trumpets fire men's hearts for fray.
No race of wild things winged or finned
May match the might that wings thy wind
Through air and sea, through scud and spray.
Strong joy and thou were powers twin-born
Of tempest and the towering morn.

APRIL

Crowned April, king whose kiss bade earth
Bring forth to time her lordliest birth
When Shakespeare from thy lips drew breath
And laughed to hold in one soft hand
A spell that bade the world's wheel stand,
And power on life, and power on death,
With quiring suns and sunbright showers
Praise him, the flower of all thy flowers.

MAY

Hail, May, whose bark puts forth full-sailed
For summer; May, whom Chaucer hailed
With all his happy might of heart,
And gave thy rosebright daisy-tips
Strange fragrance from his amorous lips
That still thine own breath seems to part
And sweeten till each word they say
Is even a flower of flowering May.

JUNE

Strong June, superb, serene, elate
With conscience of thy sovereign state
Untouched of thunder, though the storm
Scathe here and there thy shuddering skies
And bid its lightning cross thine eyes
With fire, thy golden hours inform
Earth and the souls of men with life
That brings forth peace from shining strife.

JULY

Hail, proud July, whose fervent mouth
Bids even be morn and north be south
By grace and gospel of thy word,
Whence all the splendour of the sea
Lies breathless with delight in thee
And marvel at the music heard
From the ardent silent lips of noon
And midnight's rapturous plenilune.

AUGUST

Great August, lord of golden lands,
Whose lordly joy through seas and strands
And all the red-ripe heart of earth
Strikes passion deep as life, and stills
The folded vales and folding hills
With gladness too divine for mirth,
The gracious glories of thine eyes
Make night a noon where darkness dies.

SEPTEMBER

Hail, kind September, friend whose grace
Renews the bland year's bounteous face
With largess given of corn and wine
Through many a land that laughs with love
Of thee and all the heaven above,
More fruitful found than all save thine
Whose skies fulfil with strenuous cheer
The fervent fields that knew thee near.

OCTOBER

October of the tawny crown,
Whose heavy-laden hands drop down
Blessing, the bounties of thy breath
And mildness of thy mellowing might
Fill earth and heaven with love and light
Too sweet for fear to dream of death
Or memory, while thy joy lives yet,
To know what joy would fain forget.

NOVEMBER

Hail, soft November, though thy pale
Sad smile rebuke the words that hail
Thy sorrow with no sorrowing words
Or gratulate thy grief with song
Less bitter than the winds that wrong
Thy withering woodlands, where the birds
Keep hardly heart to sing or see
How fair thy faint wan face may be.

DECEMBER

December, thou whose hallowing hands
On shuddering seas and hardening lands
Set as a sacramental sign
The seal of Christmas felt on earth
As witness toward a new year's birth
Whose promise makes thy death divine,
The crowning joy that comes of thee
Makes glad all grief on land or sea.

ENGLAND: AN ODE

I

Sea and strand, and a lordlier land than sea-tides rolling and rising sun
Clasp and lighten in climes that brighten with day when day that was here is done,
Call aloud on their children, proud with trust that future and past are one.

Far and near from the swan's nest here the storm-birds bred of her fair white breast,
Sons whose home was the sea-wave's foam, have borne the fame of her east and west;
North and south has the storm-wind's mouth rung praise of England and England's quest.

Fame, wherever her flag flew, never forbore to fly with an equal wing:
France and Spain with their warrior train bowed down before her as thrall to king;
India knelt at her feet, and felt her sway more fruitful of life than spring.

Darkness round them as iron bound fell off from races of elder name,
Slain at sight of her eyes, whose light bids freedom lighten and burn as flame;
Night endures not the touch that cures of kingship tyrants, and slaves of shame.

All the terror of time, where error and fear were lords of a world of slaves,
Age on age in resurgent rage and anguish darkening as waves on waves,
Fell or fled from a face that shed such grace as quickens the dust of graves.

Things of night at her glance took flight: the strengths of darkness recoiled and sank:
Sank the fires of the murderous pyres whereon wild agony writhed and shrank:
Rose the light of the reign of right from gulfs of years that the darkness drank.

Yet the might of her wings in flight, whence glory lightens and music rings,
Loud and bright as the dawn's, shall smite and still the discord of evil things,
Yet not slain by her radiant reign, but darkened now by her sail-stretched wings.

II

Music made of change and conquest, glory born of evil slain,
Stilled the discord, slew the darkness, bade the lights of tempest wane,
Where the deathless dawn of England rose in sign that right should reign.

Mercy, where the tiger wallowed mad and blind with blood and lust,
Justice, where the jackal yelped and fed, and slaves allowed it just,
Rose as England's light on Asia rose, and smote them down to dust.

Justice bright as mercy, mercy girt by justice with her sword,
Smote and saved and raised and ruined, till the tyrant-ridden horde
Saw the lightning fade from heaven and knew the sun for God and lord.

Where the footfall sounds of England, where the smile of England shines,
Rings the tread and laughs the face of freedom, fair as hope divines

Days to be, more brave than ours and lit by lordlier stars for signs.

All our past acclaims our future: Shakespeare's voice and Nelson's hand,
Milton's faith and Wordsworth's trust in this our chosen and chainless land,
Bear us witness: come the world against her, England yet shall stand.

Earth and sea bear England witness if he lied who said it; he
Whom the winds that ward her, waves that clasp, and herb and flower and tree
Fed with English dews and sunbeams, hail as more than man may be.

No man ever spake as he that bade our England be but true,
Keep but faith with England fast and firm, and none should bid her rue;
None may speak as he: but all may know the sign that Shakespeare knew.

III

From the springs of the dawn, from the depths of the noon, from the heights of the night that shine,
Hope, faith, and remembrance of glory that found but in England her throne and her shrine,
Speak louder than song may proclaim them, that here is the seal of them set for a sign.

And loud as the sea's voice thunders applause of the land that is one with the sea
Speaks Time in the ear of the people that never at heart was not inly free
The word of command that assures us of life, if we will but that life shall be;

If the race that is first of the races of men who behold unashamed the sun
Stand fast and forget not the sign that is given of the years and the wars that are done,
The token that all who are born of its blood should in heart as in blood be one.

The word of remembrance that lightens as fire from the steeps of the storm-lit past
Bids only the faith of our fathers endure in us, firm as they held it fast:
That the glory which was from the first upon England alone may endure to the last.

That the love and the hate may change not, the faith may not fade, nor the wrath nor scorn,
That shines for her sons and that burns for her foemen as fire of the night or the morn:
That the births of her womb may forget not the sign of the glory wherein they were born.

A light that is more than the sunlight, an air that is brighter than morning's breath,
Clothes England about as the strong sea clasps her, and answers the word that it saith;
The word that assures her of life if she change not, and choose not the ways of death.

Change darkens and lightens around her, alternate in hope and in fear to be:
Hope knows not if fear speak truth, nor fear whether hope be not blind as she:
But the sun is in heaven that beholds her immortal, and girdled with life by the sea.

ETON: AN ODE

I

Four hundred summers and fifty have shone on the meadows of Thames and died
Since Eton arose in an age that was darkness, and shone by his radiant side
As a star that the spell of a wise man's word bade live and ascend and abide.

And ever as time's flow brightened, a river more dark than the storm-clothed sea,
And age upon age rose fairer and larger in promise of hope set free,
With England Eton her child kept pace as a fostress of men to be.

And ever as earth waxed wiser, and softer the beating of time's wide wings,
Since fate fell dark on her father, most hapless and gentlest of star-crossed kings,
Her praise has increased as the chant of the dawn that the choir of the noon outsings.

II

Storm and cloud in the skies were loud, and lightning mocked at the blind sun's light;
War and woe on the land below shed heavier shadow than falls from night;
Dark was earth at her dawn of birth as here her record of praise is bright.

Clear and fair through her morning air the light first laugh of the sunlit stage
Rose and rang as a fount that sprang from depths yet dark with a spent storm's rage,
Loud and glad as a boy's, and bade the sunrise open on Shakespeare's age.

Lords of state and of war, whom fate found strong in battle, in counsel strong,
Here, ere fate had approved them great, abode their season, and thought not long:
Here too first was the lark's note nursed that filled and flooded the skies with song.

III

Shelley, lyric lord of England's lordliest singers, here first heard
Ring from lips of poets crowned and dead the Promethean word
Whence his soul took fire, and power to outsoar the sunward-soaring bird.

Still the reaches of the river, still the light on field and hill,
Still the memories held aloft as lamps for hope's young fire to fill,
Shine, and while the light of England lives shall shine for England still.

When four hundred more and fifty years have risen and shone and set,
Bright with names that men remember, loud with names that men forget,
Haply here shall Eton's record be what England finds it yet.

THE UNION

I

Three in one, but one in three,
God, who girt her with the sea,
Bade our Commonweal to be:
Nought, if now not one.
Though fraud and fear would sever
The bond assured for ever,
Their shameful strength shall never
Undo what heaven has done.

II

South and North and West and East
Watch the ravens flock to feast,
Dense as round some death-struck beast,
Black as night is black.
Stand fast as faith together
In stress of treacherous weather
When hounds and wolves break tether
And Treason guides the pack.

III

Lovelier than thy seas are strong,
Glorious Ireland, sword and song
Gird and crown thee: none may wrong,
Save thy sons alone.
The sea that laughs around us
Hath sundered not but bound us:
The sun's first rising found us
Throned on its equal throne.

IV

North and South and East and West,
All true hearts that wish thee best
Beat one tune and own one quest,
Staunch and sure as steel.
God guard from dark disunion
Our threefold State's communion,
God save the loyal Union,

The royal Commonweal!

EAST TO WEST

Sunset smiles on sunrise: east and west are one,
Face to face in heaven before the sovereign sun.
From the springs of the dawn everlasting a glory renews and transfigures the west,
From the depths of the sunset a light as of morning enkindles the broad sea's breast,
And the lands and the skies and the waters are glad of the day's and the night's work done.

Child of dawn, and regent on the world-wide sea,
England smiles on Europe, fair as dawn and free.
Not the waters that gird her are purer, nor mightier the winds that her waters know.
But America, daughter and sister of England, is praised of them, far as they flow:
Atlantic responds to Pacific the praise of her days that have been and shall be.

So from England westward let the watchword fly,
So for England eastward let the seas reply;
Praise, honour, and love everlasting be sent on the wind's wings, westward and east,
That the pride of the past and the pride of the future may mingle as friends at feast,
And the sons of the lords of the world-wide seas be one till the world's life die.

INSCRIPTIONS

FOR THE FOUR SIDES OF A PEDESTAL

I

Marlowe, the father of the sons of song
Whose praise is England's crowning praise, above
All glories else that crown her, sweet and strong
As England, clothed with light and fire of love,
And girt with might of passion, thought, and trust,
Stands here in spirit, sleeps not here in dust.

II

Marlowe, a star too sovereign, too superb,
To fade when heaven took fire from Shakespeare's light,
A soul that knew but song's triumphal curb
And love's triumphant bondage, holds of right
His pride of place, who first in place and time
Made England's voice as England's heart sublime.

III

Marlowe bade England live in living song:
The light he lifted up lit Shakespeare's way:
He spake, and life sprang forth in music, strong
As fire or lightning, sweet as dawn of day.
Song was a dream where day took night to wife:
"Let there be life," he said: and there was life.

IV

Marlowe of all our fathers first beheld
Beyond the tidal ebb and flow of things
The tideless depth and height of souls, impelled
By thought or passion, borne on waves or wings,
Beyond all flight or sight but song's: and he
First gave our song a sound that matched our sea.

ON THE DEATH OF RICHARD BURTON

Night or light is it now, wherein
Sleeps, shut out from the wild world's din,
Wakes, alive with a life more clear,
One who found not on earth his kin?

Sleep were sweet for awhile, were dear
Surely to souls that were heartless here,
Souls that faltered and flagged and fell,
Soft of spirit and faint of cheer.

A living soul that had strength to quell
Hope the spectre and fear the spell,
Clear-eyed, content with a scorn sublime
And a faith superb, can it fare not well?

Life, the shadow of wide-winged time,
Cast from the wings that change as they climb,
Life may vanish in death, and seem
Less than the promise of last year's prime.

But not for us is the past a dream
Wherefrom, as light from a clouded stream,
Faith fades and shivers and ebbs away,

Faint as the moon if the sundawn gleam.

Faith, whose eyes in the low last ray
Watch the fire that renews the day,
Faith which lives in the living past,
Rock-rooted, swerves not as weeds that sway.

As trees that stand in the storm-wind fast
She stands, unsmitten of death's keen blast,
With strong remembrance of sunbright spring
Alive at heart to the lifeless last.

Night, she knows, may in no wise cling
To a soul that sinks not and droops not wing,
A sun that sets not in death's false night
Whose kingdom finds him not thrall but king.

Souls there are that for soul's affright
Bow down and cower in the sun's glad sight,
Clothed round with faith that is one with fear,
And dark with doubt of the live world's light.

But him we hailed from afar or near
As boldest born of the bravest here
And loved as brightest of souls that eyed
Life, time, and death with unchangeful cheer,

A wider soul than the world was wide,
Whose praise made love of him one with pride,
What part has death or has time in him,
Who rode life's lists as a god might ride?

While England sees not her old praise dim,
While still her stars through the world's night swim,
A fame outshining her Raleigh's fame,
A light that lightens her loud sea's rim,

Shall shine and sound as her sons proclaim
The pride that kindles at Burton's name.
And joy shall exalt their pride to be
The same in birth if in soul the same.

But we that yearn for a friend's face—we
Who lack the light that on earth was he—
Mourn, though the light be a quenchless flame
That shines as dawn on a tideless sea.

ELEGY

1869-1891

Auvergne, Auvergne, O wild and woful land,
O glorious land and gracious, white as gleam
The stairs of heaven, black as a flameless brand,
Strange even as life, and stranger than a dream,

Could earth remember man, whose eyes made bright
The splendour of her beauty, lit by day
Or soothed and softened and redeemed by night,
Wouldst thou not know what light has passed away?

Wouldst thou not know whom England, whom the world,
Mourns? For the world whose wildest ways he trod,
And smiled their dangers down that coiled and curled
Against him, knows him now less man than god.

Our demigod of daring, keenest-eyed
To read and deepest read in earth's dim things,
A spirit now whose body of death has died
And left it mightier yet in eyes and wings,
The sovereign seeker of the world, who now
Hath sought what world the light of death may show,
Hailed once with me the crowns that load thy brow,
Crags dark as midnight, columns bright as snow.

Thy steep small Siena, splendid and content
As shines the mightier city's Tuscan pride
Which here its face reflects in radiance, pent
By narrower bounds from towering side to side,

Set fast between the ridged and foamless waves
Of earth more fierce and fluctuant than the sea,
The fearless town of towers that hails and braves
The heights that gird, the sun that brands Le Puy;

The huddled churches clinging on the cliffs
As birds alighting might for storm's sake cling,
Moored to the rocks as tempest-harried skiffs
To perilous refuge from the loud wind's wing;

The stairs on stairs that wind and change and climb
Even up to the utmost crag's edge curved and curled,
More bright than vision, more than faith sublime,
Strange as the light and darkness of the world;

Strange as are night and morning, stars and sun,
And washed from west and east by day's deep tide.
Shine yet less fair, when all their heights are won,
Than sundawn shows thy pillared mountain-side.

Even so the dawn of death, whose light makes dim
The starry fires that life sees rise and set,
Shows higher than here he shone before us him
Whom faith forgets not, nor shall fame forget.

Even so those else unfooted heights we clomb
Through scudding mist and eddying whirls of cloud,
Blind as a pilot beaten blind with foam,
And shrouded as a corpse with storm's grey shroud,

Foot following foot along the sheer strait ledge
Where space was none to bear the wild goat's feet
Till blind we sat on the outer footless edge
Where darkling death seemed fain to share the seat,

The abyss before us, viewless even as time's,
The abyss to left of us, the abyss to right,
Bid thought now dream how high the freed soul climbs
That death sets free from change of day and night.

The might of raging mist and wind whose wrath
Shut from our eyes the narrowing rock we trod,
The wondrous world it darkened, made our path
Like theirs who take the shadow of death for God.

Yet eastward, veiled in vapour white as snow,
The grim black herbless heights that scorn the sun
And mock the face of morning rose to show
The work of earth-born fire and earthquake done.

And half the world was haggard night, wherein
We strove our blind way through: but far above
Was light that watched the wild mists whirl and spin,
And far beneath a land worth light and love.

Deep down the Valley of the Curse, undaunted
By shadow and whisper of winds with sins for wings
And ghosts of crime wherethrough the heights live haunted
By present sense of past and monstrous things,

The glimmering water holds its gracious way
Full forth, and keeps one happier hand's-breadth green

Of all that storm-scathed world whereon the sway
Sits dark as death of deadlier things unseen.

But on the soundless and the viewless river
That bears through night perchance again to day
The dead whom death and twin-born fame deliver
From life that dies, and time's inveterate sway,

No shadow save of falsehood and of fear
That brands the future with the past, and bids
The spirit wither and the soul grow sere,
Hovers or hangs to cloud life's opening lids,

If life have eyes to lift again and see,
Beyond the bounds of sensual sight or breath,
What life incognisable of ours may be
That turns our light to darkness deep as death.

Priests and the soulless serfs of priests may swarm
With vulturous acclamation, loud in lies,
About his dust while yet his dust is warm
Who mocked as sunlight mocks their base blind eyes,

Their godless ghost of godhead, false and foul
As fear his dam or hell his throne: but we,
Scarce hearing, heed no carrion church-wolf's howl:
The corpse be theirs to mock; the soul is free.

Free as ere yet its earthly day was done
It lived above the coil about us curled:
A soul whose eyes were keener than the sun,
A soul whose wings were wider than the world.

We, sons of east and west, ringed round with dreams,
Bound fast with visions, girt about with fears,
Live, trust, and think by chance, while shadow seems
Light, and the wind that wrecks a hand that steers.

He, whose full soul held east and west in poise,
Weighed man with man, and creed of man's with creed,
And age with age, their triumphs and their toys,
And found what faith may read not and may read.

Scorn deep and strong as death and life, that lit
With fire the smile at lies and dreams outworn
Wherewith he smote them, showed sublime in it
The splendour and the steadfastness of scorn.

What loftier heaven, what lordlier air, what space
Illimitable, insuperable, infinite,
Now to that strong-winged soul yields ampler place
Than passing darkness yields to passing light,

No dream, no faith can tell us: hope and fear,
Whose tongues were loud of old as children's, now
From babbling fall to silence: change is here,
And death; dark furrows drawn by time's dark plough.

Still sunward here on earth its flight was bent,
Even since the man within the child began
To yearn and kindle with superb intent
And trust in time to magnify the man.

Still toward the old garden of the Sun, whose fruit
The honey-heavy lips of Sophocles
Desired and sang, wherein the unwithering root
Sprang of all growths that thought brings forth and sees

Incarnate, bright with bloom or dense with leaf
Far-shadowing, deep as depth of dawn or night:
And all were parcel of the garnered sheaf
His strenuous spirit bound and stored aright.

And eastward now, and ever toward the dawn,
If death's deep veil by life's bright hand be rent,
We see, as through the shadow of death withdrawn,
The imperious soul's indomitable ascent.

But not the soul whose labour knew not end—
But not the swordsman's hand, the crested head—
The royal heart we mourn, the faultless friend,
Burton—a name that lives till fame be dead.

A SEQUENCE OF SONNETS ON THE DEATH OF ROBERT BROWNING

I

The clearest eyes in all the world they read
With sense more keen and spirit of sight more true
Than burns and thrills in sunrise, when the dew
Flames, and absorbs the glory round it shed,
As they the light of ages quick and dead,
Closed now, forsake us: yet the shaft that slew
Can slay not one of all the works we knew,

Nor death discrown that many-laurelled head.

The works of words whose life seems lightning wrought,
And moulded of unconquerable thought,
And quickened with imperishable flame,
Stand fast and shine and smile, assured that nought
May fade of all their myriad-moulded fame,
Nor England's memory clasp not Browning's name.

December 13, 1889.

II

Death, what hast thou to do with one for whom
Time is not lord, but servant? What least part
Of all the fire that fed his living heart,
Of all the light more keen than sundawn's bloom
That lit and led his spirit, strong as doom
And bright as hope, can aught thy breath may dart
Quench? Nay, thou knowest he knew thee what thou art,
A shadow born of terror's barren womb,
That brings not forth save shadows. What art thou,
To dream, albeit thou breathe upon his brow,
That power on him is given thee,—that thy breath
Can make him less than love acclaims him now,
And hears all time sound back the word it saith?
What part hast thou then in his glory, Death?

III

A graceless doom it seems that bids us grieve:
Venice and winter, hand in deadly hand,
Have slain the lover of her sunbright strand
And singer of a stormbright Christmas Eve.
A graceless guerdon we that loved receive
For all our love, from that the dearest land
Love worshipped ever. Blithe and soft and bland,
Too fair for storm to scathe or fire to cleave,
Shone on our dreams and memories evermore
The domes, the towers, the mountains and the shore
That gird or guard thee, Venice: cold and black
Seems now the face we loved as he of yore.
We have given thee love—no stint, no stay, no lack:
What gift, what gift is this thou hast given us back?

IV

But he—to him, who knows what gift is thine,
Death? Hardly may we think or hope, when we
Pass likewise thither where to-night is he,
Beyond the irremeable outer seas that shine
And darken round such dreams as half divine
Some sunlit harbour in that starless sea
Where gleams no ship to windward or to lee,
To read with him the secret of thy shrine.

There too, as here, may song, delight, and love,
The nightingale, the sea-bird, and the dove,
Fulfil with joy the splendour of the sky
Till all beneath wax bright as all above:
But none of all that search the heavens, and try
The sun, may match the sovereign eagle's eye.

December 14.

V

Among the wondrous ways of men and time
He went as one that ever found and sought
And bore in hand the lamplike spirit of thought
To illume with instance of its fire sublime
The dusk of many a cloudlike age and clime.
No spirit in shape of light and darkness wrought,
No faith, no fear, no dream, no rapture, nought
That blooms in wisdom, nought that burns in crime,
No virtue girt and armed and helmed with light,
No love more lovely than the snows are white,
No serpent sleeping in some dead soul's tomb,
No song-bird singing from some live soul's height,
But he might hear, interpret, or illume
With sense invasive as the dawn of doom.

VI

What secret thing of splendour or of shade
Surmised in all those wandering ways wherein
Man, led of love and life and death and sin,
Strays, climbs, or cowers, allured, absorbed, afraid,
Might not the strong and sunlike sense invade
Of that full soul that had for aim to win
Light, silent over time's dark toil and din,

Life, at whose touch death fades as dead things fade?
O spirit of man, what mystery moves in thee
That he might know not of in spirit, and see
The heart within the heart that seems to strive,
The life within the life that seems to be,
And hear, through all thy storms that whirl and drive,
The living sound of all men's souls alive?

VII

He held no dream worth waking: so he said,
He who stands now on death's triumphal steep,
Awakened out of life wherein we sleep
And dream of what he knows and sees, being dead.
But never death for him was dark or dread:
"Look forth" he bade the soul, and fear not. Weep,
All ye that trust not in his truth, and keep
Vain memory's vision of a vanished head
As all that lives of all that once was he
Save that which lightens from his word: but we,
Who, seeing the sunset-coloured waters roll,
Yet know the sun subdued not of the sea,
Nor weep nor doubt that still the spirit is whole,
And life and death but shadows of the soul.

December 15.

SUNSET AND MOONRISE

NEW YEAR'S EVE, 1889

All the west, whereon the sunset sealed the dead year's glorious grave
Fast with seals of light and fire and cloud that light and fire illume,
Glows at heart and kindles earth and heaven with joyous blush and bloom,
Warm and wide as life, and glad of death that only slays to save.
As a tide-reconquered sea-rock lies aflush with the influent wave
Lies the light aflush with darkness, lapped about by lustrous gloom,
Even as life with death, and fame with time, and memory with the tomb
Where a dead man hath for vassals Fame the serf and Time the slave.

Far from earth as heaven, the steadfast light withdrawn, superb, suspense,
Burns in dumb divine expansion of illimitable flower:
Moonrise whets the shadow's edges keen as noontide: hence and thence
Glows the presence from us passing, shines and passes not the power.
Souls arise whose word remembered is as spirit within the sense:

All the hours are theirs of all the seasons: death has but his hour.

BIRTHDAY ODE

AUGUST 6, 1891

I

Love and praise, and a length of days whose shadow cast upon time is light,
Days whose sound was a spell shed round from wheeling wings as of doves in flight,
Meet in one, that the mounting sun to-day may triumph, and cast out night.

Two years more than the full fourscore lay hallowing hands on a sacred head—
Scarce one score of the perfect four uncrowned of fame as they smiled and fled:
Still and soft and alive aloft their sunlight stays though the suns be dead.

Ere we were or were thought on, ere the love that gave us to life began,
Fame grew strong with his crescent song, to greet the goal of the race they ran,
Song with fame, and the lustrous name with years whose changes acclaimed the man.

II

Soon, ere time in the rounding rhyme of choral seasons had hailed us men,
We too heard and acclaimed the word whose breath was life upon England then—
Life more bright than the breathless light of soundless noon in a songless glen.

Ah, the joy of the heartstruck boy whose ear was opened of love to hear!
Ah, the bliss of the burning kiss of song and spirit, the mounting cheer
Lit with fire of divine desire and love that knew not if love were fear!

Fear and love as of heaven above and earth enkindled of heaven were one;
One white flame, that around his name grew keen and strong as the worldwide sun;
Awe made bright with implied delight, as weft with weft of the rainbow spun.

III

He that fears not the voice he hears and loves shall never have heart to sing:
All the grace of the sun-god's face that bids the soul as a fountain spring
Bids the brow that receives it bow, and hail his likeness on earth as king.

We that knew when the sun's shaft flew beheld and worshipped, adored and heard:
Light rang round it of shining sound, whence all men's hearts were subdued and stirred:
Joy, love, sorrow, the day, the morrow, took life upon them in one man's word.

Not for him can the years wax dim, nor downward swerve on a darkening way:
Upward wind they, and leave behind such light as lightens the front of May:
Fair as youth and sublime as truth we find the fame that we hail to-day.

THRENODY

OCTOBER 6, 1892

I

Life, sublime and serene when time had power upon it and ruled its breath,
Changed it, bade it be glad or sad, and hear what change in the world's ear saith,
Shines more fair in the starrier air whose glory lightens the dusk of death.

Suns that sink on the wan sea's brink, and moons that kindle and flame and fade,
Leave more clear for the darkness here the stars that set not and see not shade
Rise and rise on the lowlier skies by rule of sunlight and moonlight swayed.

So, when night for his eyes grew bright, his proud head pillowed on Shakespeare's breast,
Hand in hand with him, soon to stand where shine the glories that death loves best,
Passed the light of his face from sight, and sank sublimely to radiant rest.

II

Far above us and all our love, beyond all reach of its voiceless praise,
Shines for ever the name that never shall feel the shade of the changeful days
Fall and chill the delight that still sees winter's light on it shine like May's.

Strong as death is the dark day's breath whose blast has withered the life we see
Here where light is the child of night, and less than visions or dreams are we:
Strong as death; but a word, a breath, a dream is stronger than death can be.

Strong as truth and superb in youth eternal, fair as the sundawn's flame
Seen when May on her first-born day bids earth exult in her radiant name,
Lives, clothed round with its praise and crowned with love that dies not, his love-lit fame.

III

Fairer far than the morning star, and sweet for us as the songs that rang
Loud through heaven from the choral Seven when all the stars of the morning sang,
Shines the song that we loved so long—since first such love in us flamed and sprang.

England glows as a sunlit rose from mead to mountain, from sea to sea,
Bright with love and with pride above all taint of sorrow that needs must be,

Needs must live for an hour, and give its rainbow's glory to lawn and lea.

Not through tears shall the new-born years behold him, crowned with applause of men,
Pass at last from a lustrous past to life that lightens beyond their ken,
Glad and dead, and from earthward led to sunward, guided of Imogen.

THE BALLAD OF MELICERTES

IN MEMORY OF THEODORE DE BANVILLE

Death, a light outshining life, bids heaven resume
Star by star the souls whose light made earth divine.
Death, a night outshining day, sees burn and bloom
Flower by flower, and sun by sun, the fames that shine
Deathless, higher than life beheld their sovereign sign.
Dead Simonides of Ceos, late restored,
Given again of God, again by man deplored,
Shone but yestereve, a glory frail as breath.
Frail? But fame's breath quickens, kindles, keeps in ward,
Life so sweet as this that dies and casts off death.

Mother's love, and rapture of the sea, whose womb
Breeds eternal life of joy that stings like brine,
Pride of song, and joy to dare the singer's doom,
Sorrow soft as sleep and laughter bright as wine,
Flushed and filled with fragrant fire his lyric line.
As the sea-shell utters, like a stricken chord,
Music uttering all the sea's within it stored,
Poet well-beloved, whose praise our sorrow saith,
So thy songs retain thy soul, and so record
Life so sweet as this that dies and casts off death.

Side by side we mourned at Gautier's golden tomb:
Here in spirit now I stand and mourn at thine.
Yet no breath of death strikes thence, no shadow of gloom,
Only light more bright than gold of the inmost mine,
Only steam of incense warm from love's own shrine.
Not the darkling stream, the sundering Stygian ford,
Not the hour that smites and severs as a sword,
Not the night subduing light that perisheth,
Smite, subdue, divide from us by doom abhorred,
Life so sweet as this that dies and casts off death.

Prince of song more sweet than honey, lyric lord,
Not thy France here only mourns a light adored,
One whose love-lit fame the world inheriteth.

Strangers too, now brethren, hail with heart's accord
Life so sweet as this that dies and casts off death.

AU TOMBEAU DE BANVILLE

La plus douce des voix qui vibraient sous le ciel
Se tait: les rossignols ailés pleurent le frère
Qui s'envole au-dessus de l'âpre et sombre terre,
Ne lui laissant plus voir que l'être essentiel,

Esprit qui chante et rit, fleur d'une âme sans fiel.
L'ombre élyséenne, où la nuit n'est que lumière,
Revoit, tout revêtu de splendeur douce et fière,
Mélicerte, poète à la bouche de miel.

Dieux exilés, passants célestes de ce monde,
Dont on entend parfois dans notre nuit profonde
Vibrer la voix, frémir les ailes, vous savez
S'il vous aima, s'il vous pleura, lui dont la vie
Et le chant rappelaient les vôtres. Recevez
L'âme de Mélicerte affranchie et ravie.

LIGHT: AN EPICEDE

TO PHILIP BOURKE MARSTON

Love will not weep because the seal is broken
That sealed upon a life beloved and brief
Darkness, and let but song break through for token
How deep, too far for even thy song's relief,
Slept in thy soul the secret springs of grief.

Thy song may soothe full many a soul hereafter,
As tears, if tears will come, dissolve despair;
As here but late, with smile more bright than laughter,
Thy sweet strange yearning eyes would seem to bear
Witness that joy might cleave the clouds of care.

Two days agone, and love was one with pity
When love gave thought wings toward the glimmering goal
Where, as a shrine lit in some darkling city,
Shone soft the shrouded image of thy soul:
And now thou art healed of life; thou art healed, and whole.

Yea, two days since, all we that loved thee pitied:
And now with wondering love, with shame of face,
We think how foolish now, how far unfitted,
Should be from us, toward thee who hast run thy race,
Pity—toward thee, who hast won the painless place;

The painless world of death, yet unbeholden
Of eyes that dream what light now lightens thine
And will not weep. Thought, yearning toward those olden
Dear hours that sorrow sees and sees not shine,
Bows tearless down before a flameless shrine:

A flameless altar here of life and sorrow
Quenched and consumed together. These were one,
One thing for thee, as night was one with morrow
And utter darkness with the sovereign sun:
And now thou seest life, sorrow, and darkness done.

And yet love yearns again to win thee hither;
Blind love, and loveless, and unworthy thee:
Here where I watch the hours of darkness wither,
Here where mine eyes were glad and sad to see
Thine that could see not mine, though turned on me.

But now, if aught beyond sweet sleep lie hidden,
And sleep be sealed not fast on dead men's sight
For ever, thine hath grace for ours forbidden,
And sees us compassed round with change and night:
Yet light like thine is ours, if love be light.

THRENODY

Watching here alone by the fire whereat last year
Sat with me the friend that a week since yet was near,
That a week has borne so far and hid so deep,
Woe am I that I may not weep,
May not yearn to behold him here.

Shame were mine, and little the love I bore him were,
Now to mourn that better he fares than love may fare
Which desires, and would not have indeed, its will,
Would not love him so worse than ill,
Would not clothe him again with care.

Yet can love not choose but remember, hearts but ache,

Eyes but darken, only for one vain thought's poor sake,
For the thought that by this hearth's now lonely side
Two fast friends, on the day he died,
Looked once more for his hand to take.

Let thy soul forgive them, and pardon heal the sin,
Though their hearts be heavy to think what then had been,
The delight that never while they live may be—
Love's communion of speech with thee,
Soul and speech with the soul therein.

O my friend, O brother, a glory veiled and marred!
Never love made moan for a life more evil-starred.
Was it envy, chance, or chance-compelling fate,
Whence thy spirit was bruised so late,
Bowed so heavily, bound so hard?

Now released, it may be,—if only love might know—
Filled and fired with sight, it beholds us blind and low
With a pity keener yet, if that may be,
Even than ever was this that we
Felt, when love of thee wrought us woe.

None may tell the depths and the heights of life and death.
What we may we give thee: a word that sorrow saith,
And that none will heed save sorrow: scarce a song.
All we may, who have loved thee long,
Take: the best we can give is breath.

A DIRGE

A bell tolls on in my heart
As though in my ears a knell
Had ceased for awhile to swell,
But the sense of it would not part
From the spirit that bears its part
In the chime of the soundless bell.

Ah dear dead singer of sorrow,
The burden is now not thine
That grief bade sound for a sign
Through the songs of the night whose morrow
Has risen, and I may not borrow
A beam from its radiant shrine.

The burden has dropped from thee

That grief on thy life bound fast;
The winter is over and past
Whose end thou wast fain to see.
Shall sorrow not comfort me
That is thine no longer—at last?

Good day, good night, and good morrow,
Men living and mourning say.
For thee we could only pray
That night of the day might borrow
Such comfort as dreams lend sorrow:
Death gives thee at last good day.

A REMINISCENCE

The rose to the wind has yielded: all its leaves
Lie strewn on the graveyard grass, and all their light
And colour and fragrance leave our sense and sight
Bereft as a man whom bitter time bereaves
Of blossom at once and hope of garnered sheaves,
Of April at once and August. Day to night
Calls wailing, and life to death, and depth to height,
And soul upon soul of man that hears and grieves.

Who knows, though he see the snow-cold blossom shed,
If haply the heart that burned within the rose,
The spirit in sense, the life of life be dead?
If haply the wind that slays with storming snows
Be one with the wind that quickens? Bow thine head,
O Sorrow, and commune with thine heart: who knows?

VIA DOLOROSA

The days of a man are threescore years and ten.
The days of his life were half a man's, whom we
Lament, and would yet not bid him back, to be
Partaker of all the woes and ways of men.
Life sent him enough of sorrow: not again
Would anguish of love, beholding him set free,
Bring back the beloved to suffer life and see
No light but the fire of grief that scathed him then.

We know not at all: we hope, and do not fear.
We shall not again behold him, late so near,

Who now from afar above, with eyes alight
And spirit enkindled, haply toward us here
Looks down unforgetful yet of days like night
And love that has yet his sightless face in sight.

February 15, 1887.

I

TRANSFIGURATION

But half a man's days—and his days were nights.
What hearts were ours who loved him, should we pray
That night would yield him back to darkling day,
Sweet death that soothes, to life that spoils and smites?
For now, perchance, life lovelier than the light's
That shed no comfort on his weary way
Shows him what none may dream to see or say
Ere yet the soul may scale those topless heights
Where death lies dead, and triumph. Haply there
Already may his kindling eyesight find
Faces of friends—no face than his more fair—
And first among them found of all his kind
Milton, with crowns from Eden on his hair,
And eyes that meet a brother's now not blind.

II

DELIVERANCE

O Death, fair Death, sole comforter and sweet,
Nor Love nor Hope can give such gifts as thine.
Sleep hardly shows us round thy shadowy shrine
What roses hang, what music floats, what feet
Pass and what wings of angels. We repeat
Wild words or mild, disastrous or divine,
Blind prayer, blind imprecation, seeing no sign
Nor hearing aught of thee not faint and fleet
As words of men or snowflakes on the wind.
But if we chide thee, saying "Thou hast sinned, thou hast sinned,
Dark Death, to take so sweet a light away
As shone but late, though shadowed, in our skies,"
We hear thine answer—"Night has given what day
Denied him: darkness hath unsealed his eyes."

III

THANKSGIVING

Could love give strength to thank thee! Love can give
Strong sorrow heart to suffer: what we bear
We would not put away, albeit this were
A burden love might cast aside and live.
Love chooses rather pain than palliative,
Sharp thought than soft oblivion. May we dare
So trample down our passion and our prayer
That fain would cling round feet now fugitive
And stay them—so remember, so forget,
What joy we had who had his presence yet,
What griefs were his while joy in him was ours
And grief made weary music of his breath,
As even to hail his best and last of hours
With love grown strong enough to thank thee, Death?

IV

LIBITINA VERTICORDIA

Sister of sleep, healer of life, divine
As rest and strong as very love may be,
To set the soul that love could set not free,
To bid the skies that day could bid not shine,
To give the gift that life withheld was thine.
With all my heart I loved one borne from me:
And all my heart bows down and praises thee,
Death, that hast now made grief not his but mine.

O Changer of men's hearts, we would not bid thee
Turn back our hearts from sorrow: this alone
We bid, we pray thee, from thy sovereign throne
And sanctuary sublime where heaven has hid thee,
Give: grace to know of those for whom we weep
That if they wake their life is sweet as sleep.

V

THE ORDER OF RELEASE

Thou canst not give it. Grace enough is ours
To know that pain for him has fallen on rest.
The worst we know was his on earth: the best,

We fain would think,—a thought no fear deflowers—
Is his, released from bonds of rayless hours.
Ah, turn our hearts from longing; bid our quest
Cease, as content with failure. This thy guest
Sleeps, vexed no more of time's imperious powers,
The spirit of hope, the spirit of change and loss,
The spirit of love bowed down beneath his cross,
Nor now needs comfort from the strength of song.
Love, should he wake, bears now no cross for him:
Dead hope, whose living eyes like his were dim,
Has brought forth better comfort, strength more strong.

VI

PSYCHAGOGOS

As Greece of old acclaimed thee God and man,
So, Death, our tongue acclaims thee: yet wast thou
Hailed of old Rome as Romans hail thee now,
Goddess and woman. Since the sands first ran
That told when first man's life and death began,
The shadows round thy blind ambiguous brow
Have mocked the votive plea, the pleading vow
That sought thee sorrowing, fain to bless or ban.

But stronger than a father's love is thine,
And gentler than a mother's. Lord and God,
Thy staff is surer than the wizard rod
That Hermes bare as priest before thy shrine
And herald of thy mercies. We could give
Nought, when we would have given: thou bidst him live.

VII

THE LAST WORD

So many a dream and hope that went and came,
So many and sweet, that love thought like to be,
Of hours as bright and soft as those for me
That made our hearts for song's sweet love the same,
Lie now struck dead, that hope seems one with shame.
O Death, thy name is Love: we know it, and see
The witness: yet for very love's sake we
Can hardly bear to mix with thine his name.

Philip, how hard it is to bid thee part

Thou knowest, if aught thou knowest where now thou art
Of us that loved and love thee. None may tell
What none but knows—how hard it is to say
The word that seals up sorrow, darkens day,
And bids fare forth the soul it bids farewell.

The wider world of men that is not ours
Receives a soul whose life on earth was light.
Though darkness close the date of human hours,
Love holds the spirit and sense of life in sight,
That may not, even though death bid fly, take flight.
Faith, love, and hope fulfilled with memory, see
As clear and dear as life could bid it be
The present soul that is and is not he.

He, who held up the shield and sword of Rome
Against the ravening brood of recreant France,
Beside the man of men whom heaven took home
When earth beheld the spring's first eyebeams glance
And life and winter seemed alike a trance
Eighteen years since, in sight of heaven and spring
That saw the soul above all souls take wing,
He too now hears the heaven we hear not sing.

He too now dwells where death is dead, and stands
Where souls like stars exult in life to be:
Whence all who linked heroic hearts and hands
Shine on our sight, and give it strength to see
What hope makes fair for all whom faith makes free:
Free with such freedom as we find in sleep,
The light sweet shadow of death, when dreams are deep
And high as heaven whence light and lightning leap.

And scarce a month yet gone, his living hand
Writ loving words that sealed me friend of his.
Are heaven and earth as near as sea to strand?
May life and death as bride and bridegroom kiss?
His last month's written word abides, and is;
Clear as the sun that lit through storm and strife
And darkling days when hope took fear to wife
The faith whose fire was light of all his life.

A life so fair, so pure of earthlier leaven,
That none hath won through higher and harder ways

The deathless life of death which earth calls heaven;
Heaven, and the light of love on earth, and praise
Of silent memory through subsiding days
Wherein the light subsides not whence the past
Feeds full with life the future. Time holds fast
Their names whom faith forgets not, first and last.

Forget? The dark forgets not dawn, nor we
The suns that sink to rise again, and shine
Lords of live years and ages. Earth and sea
Forget not heaven that makes them seem divine,
Though night put out their fires and bid their shrine
Be dark and pale as storm and twilight. Day,
Not night, is everlasting: life's full sway
Bids death bow down as dead, and pass away.

What part has death in souls that past all fear
Win heavenward their supernal way, and smite
With scorn sublime as heaven such dreams as here
Plague and perplex with cloud and fire the light
That leads men's waking souls from glimmering night
To the awless heights of day, whereon man's awe,
Transfigured, dies in rapture, seeing the law
Sealed of the sun that earth arising saw?

Faith, justice, mercy, love, and heaven-born hate
That sets them all on fire and bids them be
More than soft words and dreams that wake too late,
Shone living through the lordly life that we
Beheld, revered, and loved on earth, while he
Dwelt here, and bade our eyes take light thereof;
Light as from heaven that flamed or smiled above
In light or fire whose very hate was love.

No hate of man, but hate of hate whose foam
Sheds poison forth from tongues of snakes and priests,
And stains the sickening air with steams whence Rome
Now feeds not full the God that slays and feasts;
For now the fangs of all the ravenous beasts
That ramped about him, fain of prayer and prey,
Fulfil their lust no more: the tide of day
Swells, and compels him down the deathward way.

Night sucks the Church its creature down, and hell
Yawns, heaves, and yearns to clasp its loathliest child
Close to the breasts that bore it. All the spell
Whence darkness saw the dawn in heaven defiled
Is dumb as death: the lips that lied and smiled

Wax white for fear as ashes. She that bore
The banner up of darkness now no more
Sheds night and fear and shame from shore to shore.

When they that cast her kingdom down were born,
North cried on south and east made moan to west
For hopes that love had hardly heart to mourn,
For Italy that was not. Kings on quest,
By priests whose blessings burn as curses blest,
Made spoil of souls and bodies bowed and bound,
Hunted and harried, leashed as horse or hound,
And hopeless of the hope that died unfound.

And now that faith has brought forth fruit to time,
How should not memory praise their names, and hold
Their record even as Dante's life sublime,
Who bade his dream, found fair and false of old,
Live? Not till earth and heaven be dead and cold
May man forget whose work and will made one
Italy, fair as heaven or freedom won,
And left their fame to shine beside her sun.

April 1890.

THE FESTIVAL OF BEATRICE

Dante, sole standing on the heavenward height,
Beheld and heard one saying, "Behold me well:
I am, I am Beatrice." Heaven and hell
Kept silence, and the illimitable light
Of all the stars was darkness in his sight
Whose eyes beheld her eyes again, and fell
Shame-stricken. Since her soul took flight to dwell
In heaven, six hundred years have taken flight.

And now that heavenliest part of earth whereon
Shines yet their shadow as once their presence shone
To her bears witness for his sake, as he
For hers bare witness when her face was gone:
No slave, no hospice now for grief—but free
From shore to mountain and from Alp to sea.

THE MONUMENT OF GIORDANO BRUNO

I

Not from without us, only from within,
Comes or can ever come upon us light
Whereby the soul keeps ever truth in sight.
No truth, no strength, no comfort man may win,
No grace for guidance, no release from sin,
Save of his own soul's giving. Deep and bright
As fire enkindled in the core of night
Burns in the soul where once its fire has been
The light that leads and quickens thought, inspired
To doubt and trust and conquer. So he said
Whom Sidney, flower of England, lordliest head
Of all we love, loved: but the fates required
A sacrifice to hate and hell, ere fame
Should set with his in heaven Giordano's name.

II

Cover thine eyes and weep, O child of hell,
Grey spouse of Satan, Church of name abhorred.
Weep, withered harlot, with thy weeping lord,
Now none will buy the heaven thou hast to sell
At price of prostituted souls, and swell
Thy loveless list of lovers. Fire and sword
No more are thine: the steel, the wheel, the cord,
The flames that rose round living limbs, and fell
In lifeless ash and ember, now no more
Approve thee godlike. Rome, redeemed at last
From all the red pollution of thy past,
Acclaims the grave bright face that smiled of yore
Even on the fire that caught it round and clomb
To cast its ashes on the face of Rome.

June 9, 1889.

LIFE IN DEATH

He should have followed who goes forth before us,
Last born of us in life, in death first-born:
The last to lift up eyes against the morn,
The first to see the sunset. Life, that bore us
Perchance for death to comfort and restore us,
Of him hath left us here awhile forlorn,
For him is as a garment overworn,

And time and change, with suns and stars in chorus,
Silent. But if, beyond all change or time,
A law more just, more equal, more sublime
Than sways the surge of life's loud sterile sea
Sways that still world whose peace environs him,
Where death lies dead as night when stars wax dim,
Above all thought or hope of ours is he.

August 2, 1891.

EPICEDE

As a vesture shalt thou change them, said the prophet,
And the raiment that was flesh is turned to dust;
Dust and flesh and dust again the likeness of it,
And the fine gold woven and worn of youth is rust.
Hours that wax and wane salute the shade and scoff it,
That it knows not aught it doth nor aught it must:
Day by day the speeding soul makes haste to doff it,
Night by night the pride of life resigns its trust.

Sleep, whose silent notes of song loud life's derange not,
Takes the trust in hand awhile as angels may:
Joy with wings that rest not, grief with wings that range not,
Guard the gates of sleep and waking, gold or grey.
Joys that joys estrange, and griefs that griefs estrange not,
Day that yearns for night, and night that yearns for day,
As a vesture shalt thou change them, and they change not,
Seeing that change may never change or pass away.

Life of death makes question, "What art thou that changest?
What am I, that fear should trust or faith should doubt?
I that lighten, thou that darkenest and estrangest,
Is it night or day that girds us round about?
Light and darkness on the ways wherein thou rangest
Seem as one, and beams as clouds they put to rout.
Strange is hope, but fear of all things born were strangest,
Seeing that none may strive with change to cast it out.

"Change alone stands fast, thou sayest, O death: I know not:
What art thou, my brother death, that thou shouldst know?
Men may reap no fruits of fields wherein they sow not;
Hope or fear is all the seed we have to sow.
Winter seals the sacred springs up that they flow not:
Wind and sun and change unbind them, and they flow.
Am I thou or art thou I? The years that show not

Pass, and leave no sign when time shall be to show."

Hope makes suit to faith lest fear give ear to sorrow:
Doubt strews dust upon his head, and goes his way.
All the golden hope that life of death would borrow,
How, if death require again, may life repay?
Earth endures no darkness whence no light yearns thorough;
God in man as light in darkness lives, they say:
Yet, would midnight take assurance of the morrow,
Who shall pledge the faith or seal the bond of day?

Darkness, mute or loud with music or with mourning,
Starry darkness, winged with wind or clothed with calm,
Dreams no dream of grief or fear or wrath or warning,
Bears no sign of race or goal or strife or palm.
Word of blessing, word of mocking or of scorning,
Knows it none, nor whence its breath sheds blight or balm.
Yet a little while, and hark, the psalm of morning:
Yet a little while, and silence takes the psalm.

All the comfort, all the worship, all the wonder,
All the light of love that darkness holds in fee,
All the song that silence keeps or keeps not under,
Night, the soul that knows gives thanks for all to thee.
Far beyond the gates that morning strikes in sunder,
Hopes that grief makes holy, dreams that fear sets free,
Far above the throne of thought, the lair of thunder,
Silent shines the word whose utterance fills the sea.

MEMORIAL VERSES ON THE DEATH OF WILLIAM BELL SCOTT

A life more bright than the sun's face, bowed
Through stress of season and coil of cloud,
Sets: and the sorrow that casts out fear
Scarce deems him dead in his chill still shroud,

Dead on the breast of the dying year,
Poet and painter and friend, thrice dear
For love of the suns long set, for love
Of song that sets not with sunset here,

For love of the fervent heart, above
Their sense who saw not the swift light move
That filled with sense of the loud sun's lyre
The thoughts that passion was fain to prove

In fervent labour of high desire
And faith that leapt from its own quenched pyre
Alive and strong as the sun, and caught
From darkness light, and from twilight fire.

Passion, deep as the depths unsought
Whence faith's own hope may redeem us nought,
Filled full with ardour of pain sublime
His mourning song and his mounting thought.

Elate with sense of a sterner time,
His hand's flight clomb as a bird's might climb
Calvary: dark in the darkling air
That shrank for fear of the crowning crime,

Three crosses rose on the hillside bare,
Shown scarce by grace of the lightning's glare
That clove the veil of the temple through
And smote the priests on the threshold there.

The soul that saw it, the hand that drew,
Whence light as thought's or as faith's glance flew,
And stung to life the sepulchral past,
And bade the stars of it burn anew,

Held no less than the dead world fast
The light live shadows about them cast,
The likeness living of dawn and night,
The days that pass and the dreams that last.

Thought, clothed round with sorrow as light,
Dark as a cloud that the moon turns bright,
Moved, as a wind on the striving sea,
That yearns and quickens and flags in flight,

Through forms of colour and song that he
Who fain would have set its wide wings free
Cast round it, clothing or chaining hope
With lights that last not and shades that flee.

Scarce in song could his soul find scope,
Scarce the strength of his hand might ope
Art's inmost gate of her sovereign shrine,
To cope with heaven as a man may cope.

But high as the hope of a man may shine
The faith, the fervour, the life divine
That thrills our life and transfigures, rose

And shone resurgent, a sunbright sign,

Through shapes whereunder the strong soul glows
And fills them full as a sunlit rose
With sense and fervour of life, whose light
The fool's eye knows not, the man's eye knows.

None that can read or divine aright
The scriptures writ of the soul may slight
The strife of a strenuous soul to show
More than the craft of the hand may write.

None may slight it, and none may know
How high the flames that aspire and glow
From heart and spirit and soul may climb
And triumph; higher than the souls lie low

Whose hearing hears not the livelong rhyme,
Whose eyesight sees not the light sublime,
That shines, that sounds, that ascends and lives
Unquenched of change, unobscured of time.

A long life's length, as a man's life gives
Space for the spirit that soars and strives
To strive and soar, has the soul shone through
That heeds not whither the world's wind drives

Now that the days and the ways it knew
Are strange, are dead as the dawn's grey dew
At high midnoon of the mounting day
That mocks the might of the dawn it slew.

Yet haply may not—and haply may—
No sense abide of the dead sun's ray
Wherein the soul that outsoars us now
Rejoiced with ours in its radiant sway.

Hope may hover, and doubt may bow,
Dreaming. Haply—they dream not how—
Not life but death may indeed be dead
When silence darkens the dead man's brow.

Hope, whose name is remembrance, fed
With love that lightens from seasons fled,
Dreams, and craves not indeed to know,
That death and life are as souls that wed.

But change that falls on the heart like snow

Can chill not memory nor hope, that show
The soul, the spirit, the heart and head,
Alive above us who strive below.

AN OLD SAYING

Many waters cannot quench love,
Neither can the floods drown it.
Who shall snare or slay the white dove
Faith, whose very dreams crown it,
Gird it round with grace and peace, deep,
Warm, and pure, and soft as sweet sleep?
Many waters cannot quench love,
Neither can the floods drown it.

Set me as a seal upon thine heart,
As a seal upon thine arm.
How should we behold the days depart
And the nights resign their charm?
Love is as the soul: though hate and fear
Waste and overthrow, they strike not here.
Set me as a seal upon thine heart,
As a seal upon thine arm.

A MOSS-ROSE

If the rose of all flowers be the rarest
That heaven may adore from above,
And the fervent moss-rose be the fairest
That sweetens the summer with love,

Can it be that a fairer than any
Should blossom afar from the tree?
Yet one, and a symbol of many,
Shone sudden for eyes that could see.

In the grime and the gloom of November
The bliss and the bloom of July
Bade autumn rejoice and remember
The balm of the blossoms gone by.

Would you know what moss-rose now it may be
That puts all the rest to the blush,
The flower was the face of a baby,

The moss was a bonnet of plush.

TO A CAT

I

Stately, kindly, lordly friend,
Condescend
Here to sit by me, and turn
Glorious eyes that smile and burn,
Golden eyes, love's lustrous meed,
On the golden page I read.

All your wondrous wealth of hair,
Dark and fair,
Silken-shaggy, soft and bright
As the clouds and beams of night,
Pays my reverent hand's caress
Back with friendlier gentleness.

Dogs may fawn on all and some
As they come;
You, a friend of loftier mind,
Answer friends alone in kind.
Just your foot upon my hand
Softly bids it understand.

Morning round this silent sweet
Garden-seat
Sheds its wealth of gathering light,
Thrills the gradual clouds with might,
Changes woodland, orchard, heath,
Lawn, and garden there beneath.

Fair and dim they gleamed below:
Now they glow
Deep as even your sunbright eyes,
Fair as even the wakening skies.
Can it not or can it be
Now that you give thanks to see?

May not you rejoice as I,
Seeing the sky
Change to heaven revealed, and bid
Earth reveal the heaven it hid
All night long from stars and moon,

Now the sun sets all in tune?

What within you wakes with day
Who can say?
All too little may we tell,
Friends who like each other well,
What might haply, if we might,
Bid us read our lives aright.

II

Wild on woodland ways your sires
Flashed like fires;
Fair as flame and fierce and fleet
As with wings on wingless feet
Shone and sprang your mother, free,
Bright and brave as wind or sea.

Free and proud and glad as they,
Here to-day
Rests or roams their radiant child,
Vanquished not, but reconciled,
Free from curb of aught above
Save the lovely curb of love.

Love through dreams of souls divine
Fain would shine
Round a dawn whose light and song
Then should right our mutual wrong—
Speak, and seal the love-lit law
Sweet Assisi's seer foresaw.

Dreams were theirs; yet haply may
Dawn a day
When such friends and fellows born,
Seeing our earth as fair at morn,
May for wiser love's sake see
More of heaven's deep heart than we.

HAWTHORN DYKE

All the golden air is full of balm and bloom
Where the hawthorns line the shelving dyke with flowers.
Joyous children born of April's happiest hours,
High and low they laugh and lighten, knowing their doom

Bright as brief—to bless and cheer they know not whom,
Heed not how, but washed and warmed with suns and showers
Smile, and bid the sweet soft gradual banks and bowers
Thrill with love of sunlit fire or starry gloom.
All our moors and lawns all round rejoice; but here
All the rapturous resurrection of the year
Finds the radiant utterance perfect, sees the word
Spoken, hears the light that speaks it. Far and near,
All the world is heaven: and man and flower and bird
Here are one at heart with all things seen and heard.

THE BROTHERS

There were twa brethren fell on strife;
Sweet fruits are sair to gather:
The tane has reft his brother of life;
And the wind wears owre the heather.

There were twa brethren fell to fray;
Sweet fruits are sair to gather:
The tane is clad in a cloak of clay;
And the wind wears owre the heather.

O loud and loud was the live man's cry,
(Sweet fruits are sair to gather)
"Would God the dead and the slain were I!"
And the wind wears owre the heather.

"O sair was the wrang and sair the fray,"
(Sweet fruits are sair to gather)
"But liefer had love be slain than slay."
And the wind wears owre the heather.

"O sweet is the life that sleeps at hame,"
(Sweet fruits are sair to gather)
"But I maun wake on a far sea's faem."
And the wind wears owre the heather.

"And women are fairest of a' things fair,"
(Sweet fruits are sair to gather)
"But never shall I kiss woman mair."
And the wind wears owre the heather.

Between the birk and the aik and the thorn
(Sweet fruits are sair to gather)
He's laid his brother to lie forlorn:

And the wind wears owre the heather.

Between the bent and the burn and the broom
(Sweet fruits are sair to gather)
He's laid him to sleep till dawn of doom:
And the wind wears owre the heather.

He's tane him owre the waters wide,
(Sweet fruits are sair to gather)
Afar to fleet and afar to bide:
And the wind wears owre the heather.

His hair was yellow, his cheek was red,
(Sweet fruits are sair to gather)
When he set his face to the wind and fled:
And the wind wears owre the heather.

His banes were stark and his een were bright
(Sweet fruits are sair to gather)
When he set his face to the sea by night:
And the wind wears owre the heather.

His cheek was wan and his hair was grey
(Sweet fruits are sair to gather)
When he came back hame frae the wide world's way:
And the wind wears owre the heather.

His banes were weary, his een were dim,
(Sweet fruits are sair to gather)
And nae man lived and had mind of him:
And the wind wears owre the heather.

"O whatten a wreck wad they seek on land"
(Sweet fruits are sair to gather)
"That they houk the turf to the seaward hand?"
And the wind wears owre the heather.

"O whatten a prey wad they think to take"
(Sweet fruits are sair to gather)
"That they delve the dykes for a dead man's sake?"
And the wind wears owre the heather.

A bane of the dead in his hand he's tane;
Sweet fruits are sair to gather:
And the red blood brak frae the dead white bane.
And the wind wears owre the heather.

He's cast it forth of his auld faint hand;

Sweet fruits are sair to gather:
And the red blood ran on the wan wet sand.
And the wind wears owre the heather.

"O whatten a slayer is this," they said,
(Sweet fruits are sair to gather)
"That the straik of his hand should raise his dead?"
And the wind wears owre the heather.

"O weel is me for the sign I take"
(Sweet fruits are sair to gather)
"That now I may die for my auld sin's sake."
And the wind wears owre the heather.

"For the dead was in wait now fifty year,"
(Sweet fruits are sair to gather)
"And now shall I die for his blood's sake here."
And the wind wears owre the heather.

JACOBITE SONG

Now who will speak, and lie not,
And pledge not life, but give?
Slaves herd with herded cattle:
The dawn grows bright for battle,
And if we die, we die not;
And if we live, we live.

The faith our fathers fought for,
The kings our fathers knew,
We fight but as they fought for:
We seek the goal they sought for,
The chance they hailed and knew,
The praise they strove and wrought for,
To leave their blood as dew
On fields that flower anew.

Men live that serve the stranger;
Hounds live that huntsmen tame:
These life-days of our living
Are days of God's good giving
Where death smiles soft on danger
And life scowls dark on shame.

And what would you do other,
Sweet wife, if you were I?

And how should you be other,
My sister, than your brother,
If you were man as I,
Born of our sire and mother,
With choice to cower and fly,
And chance to strike and die?

No churl's our oldworld name is,
The lands we leave are fair:
But fairer far than these are,
But wide as all the seas are,
But high as heaven the fame is
That if we die we share.

Our name the night may swallow,
Our lands the churl may take:
But night nor death may swallow,
Nor hell's nor heaven's dim hollow,
The star whose height we take,
The star whose light we follow
For faith's unfaltering sake
Till hope that sleeps awake.

Soft hope's light lure we serve not,
Nor follow, fain to find:
Dark time's last word may smite her
Dead, ere man's falsehood blight her,
But though she die, we swerve not,
Who cast not eye behind.

Faith speaks when hope dissembles:
Faith lives when hope lies dead:
If death as life dissembles,
And all that night assembles
Of stars at dawn lie dead,
Faint hope that smiles and trembles
May tell not well for dread:
But faith has heard it said.

Now who will fight, and fly not,
And grudge not life to give?
And who will strike beside us,
If life's or death's light guide us?
For if we live, we die not,
And if we die, we live.

The sea swings owre the slants of sand,
All white with winds that drive;
The sea swirls up to the still dim strand,
Where nae man comes alive.

At the grey soft edge of the fruitless surf
A light flame sinks and springs;
At the grey soft rim of the flowerless turf
A low flame leaps and clings.

What light is this on a sunless shore,
What gleam on a starless sea?
Was it earth's or hell's waste womb that bore
Such births as should not be?

As lithe snakes turning, as bright stars burning,
They bicker and beckon and call;
As wild waves churning, as wild winds yearning,
They flicker and climb and fall.

A soft strange cry from the landward rings—
"What ails the sea to shine?"
A keen sweet note from the spray's rim springs—
"What fires are these of thine?"

A soul am I that was born on earth
For ae day's waesome span:
Death bound me fast on the bourn of birth
Ere I were christened man.

"A light by night, I fleet and fare
Till the day of wrath and woe;
On the hems of earth and the skirts of air
Winds hurl me to and fro."

"O well is thee, though the weird be strange
That bids thee flit and flee;
For hope is child of the womb of change,
And hope keeps watch with thee.

"When the years are gone, and the time is come,
God's grace may give thee grace;
And thy soul may sing, though thy soul were dumb,
And shine before God's face.

"But I, that lighten and revel and roll

With the foam of the plunging sea,
No sign is mine of a breathing soul
That God should pity me.

"Nor death, nor heaven, nor hell, nor birth
Hath part in me nor mine:
Strong lords are these of the living earth
And loveless lords of thine.

"But I that know nor lord nor life
More sure than storm or spray,
Whose breath is made of sport and strife,
Whereon shall I find stay?"

"And wouldst thou change thy doom with me,
Full fain with thee would I:
For the life that lightens and lifts the sea
Is more than earth or sky.

"And what if the day of doubt and doom
Shall save nor smite not me?
I would not rise from the slain world's tomb
If there be no more sea.

"Take he my soul that gave my soul,
And give it thee to keep;
And me, while seas and stars shall roll
Thy life that falls on sleep."

That word went up through the mirk mid sky,
And even to God's own ear:
And the Lord was ware of the keen twin cry,
And wroth was he to hear.

He's tane the soul of the unsained child
That fled to death from birth;
He's tane the light of the wan sea wild,
And bid it burn on earth.

He's given the ghaist of the babe new-born
The gift of the water-sprite,
To ride on revel from morn to morn
And roll from night to night.

He's given the sprite of the wild wan sea
The gift of the new-born man,
A soul for ever to bide and be
When the years have filled their span.

When a year was gone and a year was come,
O loud and loud cried they—
"For the lee-lang year thou hast held us dumb
Take now thy gifts away!"

O loud and lang they cried on him,
And sair and sair they prayed:
"Is the face of thy grace as the night's face grim
For those thy wrath has made?"

A cry more bitter than tears of men
From the rim of the dim grey sea;—
"Give me my living soul again,
The soul thou gavest me,
The doom and the dole of kindly men,
To bide my weird and be!"

A cry more keen from the wild low land
Than the wail of waves that roll;—
"Take back the gift of a loveless hand,
Thy gift of doom and dole,
The weird of men that bide on land;
Take from me, take my soul!"

The hands that smite are the hands that spare;
They build and break the tomb;
They turn to darkness and dust and air
The fruits of the waste earth's womb;
But never the gift of a granted prayer,
The dole of a spoken doom.

Winds may change at a word unheard,
But none may change the tides:
The prayer once heard is as God's own word;
The doom once dealt abides.

And ever a cry goes up by day,
And ever a wail by night;
And nae ship comes by the weary bay
But her shipmen hear them wail and pray,
And see with earthly sight
The twofold flames of the twin lights play
Where the sea-banks green and the sea-floods grey
Are proud of peril and fain of prey,
And the sand quakes ever; and ill fare they
That look upon that light.

DEDICATION

1893

The sea of the years that endure not
Whose tide shall endure till we die
And know what the seasons assure not,
If death be or life be a lie,
Sways hither the spirit and thither,
A waif in the swing of the sea
Whose wrecks are of memories that wither
As leaves of a tree.

We hear not and hail not with greeting
The sound of the wings of the years,
The storm of the sound of them beating,
That none till it pass from him hears:
But tempest nor calm can imperil
The treasures that fade not or fly;
Change bids them not change and be sterile,
Death bids them not die.

Hearts plighted in youth to the royal
High service of hope and of song,
Sealed fast for endurance as loyal,
And proved of the years as they throng,
Conceive not, believe not, and fear not
That age may be other than youth;
That faith and that friendship may hear not
And utter not truth.

Not yesterday's light nor to-morrow's
Gleams nearer or clearer than gleams,
Though joys be forgotten and sorrows
Forgotten as changes of dreams,
The dawn of the days unforgotten
That noon could eclipse not or slay,
Whose fruits were as children begotten
Of dawn upon day.

The years that were flowerful and fruitless,
The years that were fruitful and dark,
The hopes that were radiant and rootless,
The hopes that were winged for their mark,
Lie soft in the sepulchres fashioned
Of hours that arise and subside,

Absorbed and subdued and impassioned,
In pain or in pride.

But far in the night that entombs them
The starshine as sunshine is strong,
And clear through the cloud that resumes them
Remembrance, a light and a song,
Rings lustrous as music and hovers
As birds that impend on the sea,
And thoughts that their prison-house covers
Arise and are free.

Forgetfulness deep as a prison
Holds days that are dead for us fast
Till the sepulchre sees rearisen
The spirit whose reign is the past,
Disentrammelled of darkness, and kindled
With life that is mightier than death,
When the life that obscured it has dwindled
And passed as a breath.

But time nor oblivion may darken
Remembrance whose name will be joy
While memory forgets not to hearken,
While manhood forgets not the boy
Who heard and exulted in hearing
The songs of the sunrise of youth
Ring radiant above him, unfearing
And joyous as truth.

Truth, winged and enkindled with rapture
And sense of the radiance of yore,
Fulfilled you with power to recapture
What never might singer before—
The life, the delight, and the sorrow
Of troublous and chivalrous years
That knew not of night or of morrow,
Of hopes or of fears.

But wider the wing and the vision
That quicken the spirit have spread
Since memory beheld with derision
Man's hope to be more than his dead.
From the mists and the snows and the thunders
Your spirit has brought for us forth
Light, music, and joy in the wonders
And charms of the north.

The wars and the woes and the glories
That quicken and lighten and rain
From the clouds of its chronicled stories,
The passion, the pride, and the pain,
Whose echoes were mute and the token
Was lost of the spells that they spake,
Rise bright at your bidding, unbroken
Of ages that break.

For you, and for none of us other,
Time is not: the dead that must live
Hold commune with you as a brother
By grace of the life that you give.
The heart that was in them is in you,
Their soul in your spirit endures:
The strength of their song is the sinew
Of this that is yours.

Hence is it that life, everlasting
As light and as music, abides
In the sound of the surge of it, casting
Sound back to the surge of the tides,
Till sons of the sons of the Norsemen
Watch, hurtling to windward and lee,
Round England, unbacked of her horsemen,
The steeds of the sea.

Algernon Charles Swinburne – A Short Biography

Algernon Charles Swinburne was born at 7 Chester Street, Grosvenor Place, in London, on April 5th, 1837. He was the eldest of six children born to Captain Charles Henry Swinburne and Lady Jane Henrietta, daughter of the 3rd Earl of Ashburnham, a wealthy Northumbrian family.

Swinburne spent his early years at East Dene in Bonchurch, on the Isle of Wight. As a child, Swinburne was nervous and frail, but also imbued with a nervous energy and fearlessness almost to the point of recklessness.

He was schooled at Eton College from 1849 to 1853. It was here that he first began to write poetry. He excelled at languages and whilst still at Eton won first prizes in both French and Italian.

From Eton he moved to Oxford where he attended at Balliol College from 1856. Here he met friends to whom he became closely attached, among them Dante Gabriel Rossetti, William Morris and Edward Burne-Jones, who in 1857, were painting their Arthurian murals on the walls of the Oxford Union. At Oxford Swinburne was mentored by Benjamin Jowett, the master of Balliol College, who recognised his poetic talent and, intervening on his behalf, tried to keep him from being expelled when he celebrated the Italian patriot Orsini, and his failed attempt on the life of Napoleon III in 1858. Swinburne had to leave the Universcity for a few months due to this but returned in May, 1860 but never received a degree.

Summers were usually spent at Capheaton Hall in Northumberland, the house of his grandfather, Sir John Swinburne, 6th Baronet, who had a famous library and was himself President of the Literary and Philosophical Society in Newcastle upon Tyne.

Swinburne proudly considered himself a native of Northumberland and this is reflected in poems such as the intensely patriotic 'Northumberland' and 'Grace Darling'. He enjoyed riding across the moors and was, it was said, a daring horseman, as he moved 'through honeyed leagues of the northland border', as he remembered the Scottish border in his Recollections.

In the period from 1857 to 1860, Swinburne was one of a number of Pre-Raphaelite's who visited and became part of Lady Pauline Trevelyan's intellectual circle at Wallington Hall, a few miles west of Morpeth in Northumberland.

After leaving college, he moved to London and began his career in earnest as well as becoming a constant visitor to the Rossetti's house. To Rossetti Swinburne was his 'little Northumbrian friend', an affectionate reference to Swinburne's small stature—a mere five foot four. Whatever Swinburne lacked in height he made up for in poetic talent. However, with the burden of such great talent came the unveiling of a dark side that was to cause him pain and would, at times, threaten his very existence with all manner of self-inflicted pains through drink, drugs and sado-machoism.

In 1860 Swinburne published two verse dramas; The Queen Mother and Rosamond but it would not be until 1865 that Swinburne would achieve literary success with Atalanta in Calydon.

In 1861, Swinburne visited Menton on the French Riviera to recover from the effects of yet another period of excess use of alcohol, staying at the Villa Laurenti. From Menton, Swinburne then travelled on to Italy, where he journeyed widely.

After Elizabeth Rossetti's death from suicide in 1862, he and Rossetti moved to Tudor House at 16 Cheyne Walk in Chelsea. The stories that survive from his year with Rossetti are typical Swinburne. In one, Rossetti once had to tell him to keep down the noise — he and a boyfriend had been sliding naked down the bannisters and disturbing Rossetti's painting. He took a sardonic delight in what the critic and biographer, Cecil Lang, calls "Algernonic exaggeration": When people began to talk scathingly about his homosexuality and other sexual proclivities, he circulated a story that he had engaged in pederasty and bestiality with a monkey — and then eaten it. How many of the stories were true and how many invented is unclear. Oscar Wilde called him "a braggart in matters of vice, who had done everything he could to convince his fellow citizens of his homosexuality and bestiality without being in the slightest degree a homosexual or a bestialiser."

In December 1862, Swinburne accompanied Scott and his guests on a trip to Tynemouth. Scott writes in his memoirs that, as they walked by the sea, Swinburne declaimed the as yet unpublished 'Hymn to Proserpine' and 'Laus Veneris' in his lilting intonation, while the waves 'were running the whole length of the long level sands towards Cullercoats and sounding like far-off acclamations'.

Swinburne possessed a curious combination of frail health and strength. He was small and slightly built, but an excellent swimmer and the first to climb Culver Cliff on the Isle of Wight. He had an extremely excitable disposition: people who met him described him as a "demoniac boy" who would go skipping about the room declaiming poetry at the top of his voice. In this as in many things, moderation was not the standard for him. Excess was. Once or twice he had fits, thought to be epileptic, in public; but he made this condition much worse by drinking past excess to unconsciousness. More than once he was delivered to the door in the small of the night, dead drunk. Throughout the 1860s and '70s he rode an alcoholic cycle of dissolution, collapse, drying out at home in the country, then returning to London where he would begin the cycle all over again.

His mania for masochism, particularly flagellation, most probably started in early childhood at Eton and was encouraged by his later friendships with Richard Monckton Milnes (one of Tennyson's fellow Apostles), who introduced him to the works of the Marquis de Sade, and Richard Burton, the Victorian explorer and adventurer. Swinburne was an alcoholic and algolagniac (a desire for sexual gratification through inflicting pain on oneself or others; sadomasochism). He found life difficult, unfulfilling but still his poetic talents pushed to the fore.

Although Swinburne continued to publish some works in periodicals in 1865 he was granted recognition by both public and critics with Atalanta in Calydon written in the style of a classical Greek tragedy.

There followed "Laus Veneris" and Poems and Ballads (1866), with their sexually charged passages, absolutely decadent for polite Victorian society, which were attacked all the more violently as a result. The poems written in homage of Sappho of Lesbos such as "Anactoria" and "Sapphics" were especially savaged. The volume also contained poems such as "The Leper," "Laus Veneris," and "St Dorothy" which evoke both Swinburne's and a general Victorian fascination with the Middle Ages, and are explicitly mediaeval in style, tone and construction. With its publication came instant notoriety. He was now identified with indecent and decadent themes and the precept of art for art's sake.

Swinburne's meeting in 1867 with his long-time hero Mazzini, the Italian patriot living in England in exile, was the beginning of a poetical journey that now became more serious and more engaged with serious thought, initially leading to the political poems in the volume Songs Before Sunrise.

Also in 1867 he was introduced to Adah Isaacs Menken, the American actress, poet and circus rider, whose main fame seemed to be riding naked on a horse (in fact she wore tight nude coloured clothing) for her performance in the melodrama Mazeppa (itself based on a poem by Lord Byron). Although they had a short affair Adah's quote implies that Swinburne was not ready for a relationship that did not involve some self-sabotage; "I can't make him understand that biting's no use."

In 1879, with Swinburne nearly dead from alcoholism and dissolution, his legal advisor Theodore Watts-Dunton took him in, and was gradually successful in getting him to adapt to a healthier lifestyle. Swinburne lived the rest of his life at Watts-Dunton's house. He saw less and less of his old bohemian friends, who thought him a prisoner at The Pines, but his growing deafness also accounts for some of his decreased sociability. By now Swinburne was 42, and was moving from a young man of rebelliousness to a figure of social respectability. It was said of Watts-Dunton that he saved the man and killed the poet.

It is clear that Swinburne had an addictive personality, and clearly incapable of moderation in his pursuit of any chosen vices. This, of course, would both nourish and perhaps sabotage his poetic career. His poetry follows the somewhat clichéd pattern of early flourish and later decline; indeed some of the fresher pieces in the second and third series of Poems and Ballads (published in 1878 and 1889) were actually written during his days at Oxford. Nevertheless, his last collection, A Channel Passage, has some beautiful poems, including "The Lake of Gaube."

He is best remembered as the supreme technician in metre, with a versatility which exceeds even Tennyson's, but which lacks a corresponding emotional range. His obsessions are not widely enough shared; and if he cannot shock us by the strangeness of his desires nor the shrillness of his anti-theistical exclamations, often what remains is not enough to fully engage with the audience.

Swinburne is considered a poet of the decadent school, although he perhaps professed to more vice than he actually indulged in to advertise his deviance. Common gossip of the time reported that he also had a deep crush on the explorer Sir Richard Francis Burton, despite the fact that Swinburne himself abhorred travel. Fact and fiction are easily absorbed by the other so are difficult to untangle even now.

Many critics consider his mastery of vocabulary, rhyme and metre impressive, although he has also been criticised for his florid style and word choices that only fit the rhyme scheme rather than contributing to the meaning of the piece. A. E. Housman, although a critic, had great praise for his rhyming ability: to Swinburne the sonnet was child's play: the task of providing four rhymes was not hard enough, and he wrote long poems in which each stanza required eight or ten rhymes, and wrote them so that he never seemed to be saying anything for the rhyme's sake.

Throughout his career Swinburne published literary criticism of great worth. His deep knowledge of world literatures contributed to a critical style rich in quotation, allusion, and comparison. He is particularly noted for discerning studies of Elizabethan dramatists and of many English and French poets and novelists. As well he was a noted essayist and wrote two novels.

Swinburne was nominated for the Nobel Prize in Literature every year from 1903 to 1907 and then again in 1909.

H.P. Lovecraft, the master of the dark side and a decent poet himself, considered Swinburne "the only real poet in either England or America after the death of Mr. Edgar Allan Poe."

Swinburne was also responsible for devising a poetic form called the roundel, a variation of the French Rondeau form. In 1883 he published A Century of Roundels with several of the roundels dedicated to Dante's sister, the poet Christina Georgina Rossetti. Swinburne wrote to Edward Burne-Jones in 1883: "I have got a tiny new book of songs or songlets, in one form and all manner of metres ... just coming out, of which Miss Rossetti has accepted the dedication. I hope you and Georgie [his wife Georgiana] will find something to like among a hundred poems of nine lines each, twenty-four of which are about babies or small children".

Opinions of the Roundel poems move between those who find them captivating and brilliant, to others who find them merely clever and contrived. One of them, A Baby's Death, was set to music by the English composer Sir Edward Elgar as the song "Roundel: The little eyes that never knew Light".

After the first Poems and Ballads, Swinburne's later poetry was devoted more to philosophy and politics, including the unification of Italy, particularly in the volume Songs before Sunrise. He did not stop writing love poetry entirely, indeed it was only in 1882 that his great epic-length poem, Tristram of Lyonesse, was published, its contents lyrical rather than shocking. His versification, and especially his rhyming technique, remain of high quality to the end.

Algernon Charles Swinburne died of influenza, at the Pines in London on April 10th, 1909 at the age of 72. He was buried at St. Boniface Church, Bonchurch on the Isle of Wight.

Algernon Charles Swinburne – A Concise Bibliography

Verse Drama
The Queen Mother (1860)
Rosamond (1860)
Chastelard (1865)
Bothwell (1874)
Mary Stuart (1881)
Marino Faliero (1885)
Locrine (1887)
The Sisters (1892)
Rosamund, Queen of the Lombards (1899)

Poetry
Atalanta in Calydon (1865)*
Poems and Ballads (1866)
Songs Before Sunrise (1871)
Songs of Two Nations (1875)
Erechtheus (1876)*
Poems and Ballads, Second Series (1878)
Songs of the Springtides (1880)
Studies in Song (1880)
The Heptalogia, or the Seven against Sense. A Cap with Seven Bells (1880)
Tristram of Lyonesse (1882)
A Dark Month & Other Poems
A Century of Roundels (1883)
A Midsummer Holiday and Other Poems (1884)
Poems and Ballads, Third Series (1889)
Astrophel and Other Poems (1894)
The Tale of Balen (1896)
A Channel Passage and Other Poems (1904)

*Although formally tragedies, Atlanta in Calydon and Erechtheus are traditionally included with his poetry.

Criticism
William Blake: A Critical Essay (1868, new edition 1906)
Under the Microscope (1872)
George Chapman: A Critical Essay (1875)
Essays and Studies (1875)
A Note on Charlotte Brontë (1877)
A Study of Shakespeare (1880)

A Study of Victor Hugo (1886)
A Study of Ben Johnson (1889)
Studies in Prose and Poetry (1894)
The Age of Shakespeare (1908)
Shakespeare (1909)

Major Collections

The Poems of Algernon Charles Swinburne, 6 vols. 1904.
The Tragedies of Algernon Charles Swinburne, 5 vols. 1905.
The Complete Works of Algernon Charles Swinburne, 20 vols. Bonchurch Edition. 1925-7.
The Swinburne Letters, 6 vols. 1959-62.

www.ingramcontent.com/pod-product-compliance
Lightning Source LLC
Chambersburg PA
CBHW060140050426
42448CB00010B/2221